The Valley of Vision

BY THE SAME AUTHOR

Rural Evangelism
Table and Ministry

The Valley of Vision

A collection of Puritan prayers and devotions

EDITED BY

ARTHUR BENNETT

Canon of St Albans Cathedral

The burden of the valley of vision
ISAIAH 22:1

The Banner of Truth Trust

THE BANNER OF TRUTH TRUST
3 Murrayfield Road, Edinburgh EH12 6EL
P.O. Box 621, Carlisle, Pennsylvania 17013, USA

© The Banner of Truth Trust 1975
First published 1975
Reprinted 1977
Reprinted 1983
Reprinted 1986
Reprinted 1989
Reprinted 1994
Reprinted 1995
Reprinted 1997
Reprinted 1999
Reprinted 2001
Reprinted 2002

ISBN 0 85151 228 3

Printed in Finland by
WS Bookwell

TO MY COLLEAGUES AND STUDENTS
AT ALL NATIONS CHRISTIAN COLLEGE, WARE,
FOR TEN YEARS' FELLOWSHIP
IN CHRIST

Preface

These prayers are drawn from the largely forgotten deposit of Puritan spiritual exercises, meditations and aspirations. They testify to the richness and colour of evangelical thought and language that animated vital piety in an important stream of English religious life. It is hoped that their publication will help to redress the neglect of this vast ocean of Puritan spirituality.

The Puritan Movement was a religious phenomenon of the sixteenth and seventeenth centuries, yet its influence continued at least to the time of Charles Haddon Spurgeon [1834–1892] who may be regarded as the last of the great Puritans. Although the political storm ended in 1660, its theological ground-swell carried forward distinct forms of practical religion for many decades, particularly family worship and private devotion. In these spheres, and in that of the authority of Scripture over the whole of life, New England Presbyterians and Congregationalists were at one with English Dissenters and Anglican evangelicals in a close-knit union that transcended differences of worship, discipline and polity. They spoke the same spiritual language, shared the same code of values, adopted the same attitude towards the Christian religion, and breathed out the same God-centred aspirations in a manner that makes it impossible to distinguish the voice of conformist from that of non-conformist. Thus, this book of Puritan prayers has a unity not often found in similar works.

The strength of Puritan character and life lay in the practice of prayer and meditation. Many of those who held the doctrines of grace wrote down a record of God's intimate dealings with their souls, not with an eye to publication, but, as in David Brainerd's case, to test their spiritual growth, and to encourage themselves by their re-perusal in times of low spiritual fervour. Others, like William Jay and Henry Law, turned their personal devotions into corporate forms for family worship, and published them to the church at large. Yet others, such as Philip Doddridge and William Romaine, wrote prayers into their literary works in order to evoke the reader's spiritual response. Many ministers went further and advised their congregations to put their private prayer thoughts on paper and vocalize them. There thus emerged an important corpus of inspiring Puritan prayers that are still largely unused.

In extracting this selection from Puritan literature it has been necessary to change some prayers from the plural and the third person into the singular and the first person in order that the book might be used chiefly in private devotion. But, by a change of pronoun, most of them can be employed in corporate worship. A final section has been added for pluralistic occasions. Old idiom has been retained, but it has been necessary to reframe some phrases in order to accommodate archaic thought to modern understanding. A number of prayers were originally spiritual experiences, as in the case of Thomas Shepard, and some others are conflations from different sources to bind together a given theme.

A poetic form has been adopted throughout as an aid to easier comprehension and utterance. Each prayer consists of a number of main clauses with subsidiaries that illuminate and enlarge the subject. In this way an opportunity is provided for pauses and reflections. The editor is thus responsible for the structure of the prayers as here printed.

The book is not intended to be read as a prayer manual. The soul learns to pray by praying; for prayer is communion with a transcendent and immanent God who on the ground of his nature and attributes calls forth all the powers of the redeemed soul in acts of total adoration and dedication. The prayers should therefore be used as aspiration units, the several parts of which could become springboards for the individual's own prayer subjects. These and their divisions can also serve homiletic purposes.

The prayers are taken from the works of Thomas Shepard, Thomas Watson, Richard Baxter, John Bunyan, Isaac Watts, William Williams, Philip Doddridge, William Romaine, David Brainerd, Augustus Toplady, Christmas Evans, William Jay, Henry Law, and Charles Haddon Spurgeon. They are sent out with the prayer of Philip Doddridge, that 'However weak and contemptible this work may seem in the eyes of the children of this world, and however imperfect it really be, it may nevertheless live before thee, and through a divine power be mighty to produce the rise and progress of religion.'

I desire to thank the Rev Iain Murray B.A. of the Banner of Truth Trust for his encouragement to produce this work, Mr S. M. Houghton M.A. many of whose kindly criticisms have been accepted, and the Rev R. E. Davies B.D., M.TH., who helped to resolve theological points. I am grateful to the Trustees of the British Museum, Dr Williams' Library, and the Evangelical Library for access to out-of-print books.

ARTHUR BENNETT

Contents

III: PENITENCE AND DEPRECATION

IV: NEEDS AND DEVOTIONS

V: HOLY ASPIRATIONS

VI: APPROACH TO GOD

VII: GIFTS OF GRACE

VIII: SERVICE AND MINISTRY

IX: VALEDICTION

X: A WEEK'S SHARED PRAYERS

Introductory

THE VALLEY OF VISION

THE VALLEY OF VISION

LORD, HIGH AND HOLY, MEEK AND LOWLY,
Thou hast brought me to the valley of vision,
    where I live in the depths but see thee in the heights;
    hemmed in by mountains of sin I behold thy glory.

Let me learn by paradox
    that the way down is the way up,
    that to be low is to be high,
    that the broken heart is the healed heart,
    that the contrite spirit is the rejoicing spirit,
    that the repenting soul is the victorious soul,
    that to have nothing is to possess all,
    that to bear the cross is to wear the crown,
    that to give is to receive,
    that the valley is the place of vision.
Lord, in the daytime stars can be seen from deepest wells,
    and the deeper the wells the brighter thy stars shine;
Let me find thy light in my darkness,
          thy life in my death,
          thy joy in my sorrow,
          thy grace in my sin,
          thy riches in my poverty,
          thy glory in my valley.

I

Father, Son, and Holy Spirit

THE TRINITY

THREE IN ONE, ONE IN THREE, GOD OF MY SALVATION,
Heavenly Father, blessed Son, eternal Spirit,
   I adore thee as one Being, one Essence,
                one God in three distinct Persons,
   for bringing sinners to thy knowledge and to thy kingdom.
O Father, thou hast loved me and sent Jesus to redeem me;
O Jesus, thou hast loved me and assumed my nature,
               shed thine own blood to wash away my sins,
               wrought righteousness to cover my unworthiness;
O Holy Spirit, thou hast loved me and entered my heart,
               implanted there eternal life,
               revealed to me the glories of Jesus.
Three Persons and one God, I bless and praise thee,
   for love so unmerited, so unspeakable, so wondrous,
   so mighty to save the lost and raise them to glory.
O Father, I thank thee that in fullness of grace
   thou hast given me to Jesus,
   to be his sheep, jewel, portion;
O Jesus, I thank thee that in fullness of grace
   thou hast accepted, espoused, bound me;
O Holy Spirit, I thank thee that in fullness of grace
   thou hast exhibited Jesus as my salvation,
             implanted faith within me,
             subdued my stubborn heart,
             made me one with him for ever.
O Father, thou art enthroned to hear my prayers,
O Jesus, thy hand is outstretched to take my petitions,
O Holy Spirit, thou art willing to help my infirmities,
   to show me my need, to supply words, to pray within me,
   to strengthen me that I faint not in supplication.
O Triune God, who commandeth the universe,
   thou hast commanded me to ask for those things
   that concern thy kingdom and my soul.
Let me live and pray as one baptized into the threefold Name.

GOD THE ALL

O GOD WHOSE WILL CONQUERS ALL,
There is no comfort in anything
    apart from enjoying thee
    and being engaged in thy service;
Thou art All in all, and all enjoyments are what to me
    thou makest them, and no more.
I am well pleased with thy will, whatever it is,
    or should be in all respects,
And if thou bidst me decide for myself in any affair
    I would choose to refer all to thee,
    for thou art infinitely wise and cannot do amiss,
    as I am in danger of doing.
I rejoice to think that all things are at thy disposal,
    and it delights me to leave them there.
Then prayer turns wholly into praise,
    and all I can do is to adore and bless thee.
What shall I give thee for all thy benefits?
    I am in a strait betwixt two, knowing not what to do;
I long to make some return, but have nothing to offer,
    and can only rejoice that thou doest all,
    that none in heaven or on earth shares thy honour;
    I can of myself do nothing to glorify thy blessed name,
    but I can through grace cheerfully surrender soul and body to thee,
I know that thou art the author and finisher of faith,
    that the whole work of redemption is thine alone,
    that every good work or thought found in me
      is the effect of thy power and grace,
    that thy sole motive in working in me to will and to do
      is for thy good pleasure.
O God, it is amazing that men can talk so much
    about man's creaturely power and goodness,
    when, if thou didst not hold us back every moment,
    we should be devils incarnate.
This, by bitter experience, thou hast taught me concerning myself.

GOD THE SOURCE OF ALL GOOD

O LORD GOD, WHO INHABITEST ETERNITY,
The heavens declare thy glory,
The earth thy riches,
The universe is thy temple;
Thy presence fills immensity,
Yet thou hast of thy pleasure created life, and communicated
   happiness;
Thou hast made me what I am, and given me what I have;
In thee I live and move and have my being;
Thy providence has set the bounds of my habitation,
    and wisely administers all my affairs.
I thank thee for thy riches to me in Jesus,
        for the unclouded revelation of him in thy Word,
           where I behold his person, character, grace, glory,
             humiliation, sufferings, death, and resurrection;
Give me to feel a need of his continual saviourhood,
    and cry with Job, 'I am vile',
        with Peter, 'I perish',
          with the publican, 'Be merciful to me, a sinner'.
Subdue in me the love of sin,
Let me know the need of renovation as well as of forgiveness,
    in order to serve and enjoy thee for ever.
I come to thee in the all-prevailing name of Jesus,
    with nothing of my own to plead,
      no works, no worthiness, no promises.
I am often straying,
    often knowingly opposing thy authority,
    often abusing thy goodness;
Much of my guilt arises from my religious privileges,
    my low estimation of them,
    my failure to use them to my advantage,
But I am not careless of thy favour or regardless of thy glory;
Impress me deeply with a sense of thine omnipresence,
    that thou art about my path, my ways, my lying down, my end.

THE GREAT GOD

O FOUNTAIN OF ALL GOOD,
Destroy in me every lofty thought,
Break pride to pieces and scatter it to the winds,
Annihilate each clinging shred of self-righteousness,
Implant in me true lowliness of spirit,
Abase me to self-loathing and self-abhorrence,
Open in me a fount of penitential tears,
Break me, then bind me up;
Thus will my heart be a prepared dwelling for my God;
  Then can the Father take up his abode in me,
  Then can the blessed Jesus come with healing in his touch,
  Then can the Holy Spirit descend in sanctifying grace;
O Holy Trinity, three Persons and one God,
  inhabit me, a temple consecrated to thy glory.
When thou art present, evil cannot abide;
In thy fellowship is fullness of joy,
Beneath thy smile is peace of conscience,
By thy side no fears disturb,
  no apprehensions banish rest of mind,
With thee my heart shall bloom with fragrance;
Make me meet, through repentance, for thine indwelling.
Nothing exceeds thy power,
Nothing is too great for thee to do,
Nothing too good for thee to give.
  Infinite is thy might, boundless thy love,
  limitless thy grace, glorious thy saving name.
Let angels sing for sinners repenting, prodigals restored,
  backsliders reclaimed, Satan's captives released,
  blind eyes opened, broken hearts bound up,
  the despondent cheered, the self-righteous stripped,
  the formalist driven from a refuge of lies,
  the ignorant enlightened,
  and saints built up in their holy faith.

I ask great things of a great God.

THE ALL-GOOD

MY GOD,
Thou hast helped me to see,
    that whatever good be in honour and rejoicing,
      how good is he who gives them, and can withdraw them;
    that blessedness does not lie so much
      in receiving good from and in thee, but
        in holding forth thy glory and virtue:
    that it is an amazing thing
        to see Deity in a creature, speaking, acting,
        filling, shining through it;
    that nothing is good but thee,
    that I am near good when I am near thee,
    that to be like thee is a glorious thing:
This is my magnet, my attraction.

Thou art all my good in times of peace,
    my only support in days of trouble,
    my one sufficiency when life shall end.
Help me to see how good thy will is in all,
    and even when it crosses mine
    teach me to be pleased with it.
Grant me to feel thee in fire, and food and every providence,
    and to see that thy many gifts and creatures
    are but thy hands and fingers taking hold of me.
Thou bottomless fountain of all good,
    I give myself to thee out of love,
      for all I have or own is thine,
      my goods, family, church, self,
    to do with as thou wilt,
    to honour thyself by me, and by all mine.
If it be consistent with thy eternal counsels,
      the purpose of thy grace,
      and the great ends of thy glory,
    then bestow upon me the blessings of thy comforts;
If not, let me resign myself to thy wiser determinations.

THE MOVER

O SUPREME MOVING CAUSE,
May I always be subordinate to thee,
   be dependent upon thee,
    be found in the path where thou dost walk,
     and where thy Spirit moves,
    take heed of estrangement from thee,
     of becoming insensible to thy love.
Thou dost not move men like stones,
  but dost endue them with life,
  not to enable them to move without thee,
  but in submission to thee, the first mover.
O Lord, I am astonished at the difference
  between my receivings and my deservings,
  between the state I am now in and my past gracelessness,
  between the heaven I am bound for and the hell I merit.
Who made me to differ, but thee?
  for I was no more ready to receive Christ than were others;
I could not have begun to love thee hadst thou not first loved me,
  or been willing unless thou hadst first made me so.
O that such a crown should fit the head of such a sinner!
  such high advancement be for an unfruitful person!
  such joys for so vile a rebel!
Infinite wisdom cast the design of salvation
  into the mould of purchase and freedom;
Let *wrath deserved* be written on the door of hell,
But *the free gift of grace* on the gate of heaven.
I know that my sufferings are the result of my sinning,
  but in heaven both shall cease;
Grant me to attain this haven and be done with sailing,
  and may the gales of thy mercy blow me safely into harbour.
Let thy love draw me nearer to thyself,
   wean me from sin, mortify me to this world,
   and make me ready for my departure hence.
Secure me by thy grace as I sail across this stormy sea.

THE DIVINE WILL

O LORD,
I hang on thee; I see, believe, live,
    when thy will, not mine, is done;
I can plead nothing in myself
    in regard of any worthiness and grace,
    in regard of thy providence and promises,
    but only thy good pleasure.
If thy mercy make me poor and vile, blessed be thou!
Prayers arising from my needs are preparations for future mercies;
Help me to honour thee by believing before I feel,
    for great is the sin if I make feeling a cause of faith.

Show me what sins hide thee from me
    and eclipse thy love;
Help me to humble myself for past evils,
    to be resolved to walk with more care,
For if I do not walk holily before thee,
    how can I be assured of my salvation?

It is the meek and humble who are shown thy covenant,
    know thy will, are pardoned and healed,
    who by faith depend and rest upon grace,
    who are sanctified and quickened,
    who evidence thy love.
Help me to pray in faith and so find thy will,
    by leaning hard on thy rich free mercy,
    by believing thou wilt give what thou hast promised;
Strengthen me to pray with the conviction
    that whatever I receive is thy gift,
    so that I may pray until prayer be granted;
Teach me to believe that all degrees of mercy arise
    from several degrees of prayer,
    that when faith is begun it is imperfect and must grow,
    as chapped ground opens wider and wider until rain comes.

So shall I wait thy will, pray for it to be done,
    and by thy grace become fully obedient.

DIVINE MERCIES

THOU ETERNAL GOD,
Thine is surpassing greatness, unspeakable goodness,
　　super-abundant grace;
I can as soon count the sands of ocean's 'lip' as number thy favours
　　towards me;
I know but a part, but that part exceeds all praise.
I thank thee for personal mercies,
　　measure of health, preservation of body,
　　comforts of house and home, sufficiency of food and clothing,
　　continuance of mental powers,
　　my family, their mutual help and support,
　　　　the delights of domestic harmony and peace,
　　　　the seats now filled that might have been vacant,
　　my country, church, Bible, faith.
But, O, how I mourn my sin, ingratitude, vileness,
　　the days that add to my guilt,
　　the scenes that witness my offending tongue;
All things in heaven, earth, around, within, without, condemn me—
　　the sun which sees my misdeeds,
　　the darkness which is light to thee,
　　the cruel accuser who justly charges me,
　　the good angels who have been provoked to leave me,
　　thy countenance which scans my secret sins,
　　thy righteous law, thy holy Word,
　　my sin-soiled conscience, my private and public life,
　　my neighbours, myself-
　　　　　　all write dark things against me.
I deny them not, frame no excuse, but confess, 'Father, I have sinned'.
Yet still I live, and fly repenting to thy outstretched arms;
　　thou wilt not cast me off, for Jesus brings me near,
　　thou wilt not condemn me, for he died in my stead,
　　thou wilt not mark my mountains of sin, for he levelled all,
　　and his beauty covers my deformities.
O my God, I bid farewell to sin by clinging to his cross,
　　hiding in his wounds, and sheltering in his side.

GOD ENJOYED

THOU INCOMPREHENSIBLE BUT PRAYER-HEARING GOD,
Known, but beyond knowledge,
revealed, but unrevealed,
    my wants and welfare draw me to thee,
    for thou hast never said, 'Seek ye me in vain'.
To thee I come in my difficulties, necessities, distresses;
    possess me with thyself,
              with a spirit of grace and supplication,
              with a prayerful attitude of mind,
              with access into warmth of fellowship,
    so that in the ordinary concerns of life
        my thoughts and desires may rise to thee,
    and in habitual devotion I may find a resource that will
        soothe my sorrows, sanctify my successes,
        and qualify me in all ways for dealings with my fellow men.

I bless thee that thou hast made me capable
    of knowing thee, the author of all being,
    of resembling thee, the perfection of all excellency,
    of enjoying thee, the source of all happiness.
O God, attend me in every part of my arduous and trying pilgrimage;
    I need the same counsel, defence, comfort I found at my beginning.
Let my religion be more obvious to my conscience,
              more perceptible to those around.
While Jesus is representing me in heaven, may I reflect him on earth,
While he pleads my cause, may I show forth his praise.

Continue the gentleness of thy goodness towards me,
And whether I wake or sleep, let thy presence go with me,
    thy blessing attend me.
Thou hast led me on and I have found thy promises true,
I have been sorrowful, but thou hast been my help,
        fearful, but thou hast delivered me,
        despairing, but thou hast lifted me up.
Thy vows are ever upon me,
    And I praise thee, O God.

A PRESENT SALVATION

CREATOR AND REDEEMER GOD,
Author of all existence, source of all blessedness,
I adore thee for making me capable of knowing thee,
       for giving me reason and conscience,
       for leading me to desire thee;
I praise thee for the revelation of thyself in the gospel,
       for thy heart as a dwelling place of pity,
       for thy thoughts of peace towards me,
       for thy patience and thy graciousness,
       for the vastness of thy mercy.
Thou hast moved my conscience to know how
    the guilty can be pardoned,
    the unholy sanctified,
    the poor enriched.
May I be always amongst those who not only hear but know thee,
    who walk with and rejoice in thee,
    who take thee at thy word and find life there.
Keep me always longing
    for a present salvation in Holy Spirit comforts and rejoicings,
    for spiritual graces and blessings,
    for help to value my duties as well as my privileges.
May I cherish simplicity and godly sincerity of character.
Help me to be in reality before thee
      as in appearance I am before men,
    to be religious before I profess religion,
    to leave the world before I enter the church,
    to set my affections on things above,
    to shun forbidden follies and vanities,
    to be a dispenser as well as a partaker of grace,
    to be prepared to bear evil as well as to do good.
O God, make me worthy of this calling,
    that the name of Jesus may be glorified in me and I in him.

MAN'S GREAT END

LORD OF ALL BEING,
There is one thing that deserves my greatest care,
                that calls forth my ardent desires,
That is, that I may answer the great end for which I am made—
    to glorify thee who hast given me being,
    and to do all the good I can for my fellow men;
Verily life is not worth having
    if it be not improved for this noble purpose.
Yet, Lord, how little is this the thought of mankind!
Most men seem to live for themselves,
    without much or any regard for thy glory,
    or for the good of others;
They earnestly desire and eagerly pursue
    the riches, honours, pleasures of this life,
    as if they supposed that wealth, greatness, merriment,
    could make their immortal souls happy;
But, alas, what false delusive dreams are these!
And how miserable ere long will those be that sleep in them,
    for all our happiness consists in loving thee,
    and being holy as thou art holy.

O may I never fall into the tempers and vanities,
    the sensuality and folly of the present world!
It is a place of inexpressible sorrow, a vast empty nothingness;
Time is a moment, a vapour,
    and all its enjoyments are empty bubbles,
    fleeting blasts of wind,
    from which nothing satisfactory can be derived;
Give me grace always to keep in covenant with thee,
    and to reject as delusion a great name here or hereafter,
    together with all sinful pleasures or profits.
Help me to know continually
    that there can be no true happiness,
    no fulfilling of thy purpose for me,
    apart from a life lived in and for the Son of thy love.

O GOD,
Praise waiteth for thee,
    and to render it is my noblest exercise;
This is thy due from all thy creatures,
    for all thy works display thy attributes and fulfil thy designs;
The sea, dry land, winter cold, summer heat,
    morning light, evening shade are full of thee,
    and thou givest me them richly to enjoy.
Thou art king of kings and lord of lords;
At thy pleasure empires rise and fall;
All thy works praise thee and thy saints bless thee;
    Let me be numbered with thy holy ones,
    resemble them in character and condition,
    sit with them at Jesus' feet.
May my religion be always firmly rooted in thy Word,
    my understanding divinely informed,
    my affections holy and heavenly,
    my motives simple and pure,
    and my heart never wrong with thee.
Deliver me from the natural darkness of my own mind,
    from the corruptions of my heart,
    from the temptations to which I am exposed,
    from the daily snares that attend me.
I am in constant danger while I am in this life;
Let thy watchful eye ever be upon me for my defence,
Save me from the power of my worldly and spiritual enemies
    and from all painful evils to which I have exposed myself.
Until the day of life dawns above
    let there be unrestrained fellowship with Jesus;
Until fruition comes, may I enjoy the earnest of my inheritance,
    and the firstfruits of the Spirit;
Until I finish my course with joy may I pursue it with diligence,
    in every part display the resources of the Christian,
    and adorn the doctrine of thee my God in all things.

PRAISE AND THANKSGIVING

O MY GOD,
Thou fairest, greatest, first of all objects,
   my heart admires, adores, loves thee,
   for my little vessel is as full as it can be,
   and I would pour out all that fullness before thee
                in ceaseless flow.
When I think upon and converse with thee
   ten thousand delightful thoughts spring up,
   ten thousand sources of pleasure are unsealed,
   ten thousand refreshing joys spread over my heart,
   crowding into every moment of happiness.
I bless thee for the soul thou hast created,
         for adorning it, sanctifying it,
           though it is fixed in barren soil;
         for the body thou hast given me,
         for preserving its strength and vigour,
         for providing senses to enjoy delights,
         for the ease and freedom of my limbs,
         for hands, eyes, ears that do thy bidding;
         for thy royal bounty providing my daily support,
         for a full table and overflowing cup,
         for appetite, taste, sweetness,
         for social joys of relatives and friends,
         for ability to serve others,
         for a heart that feels sorrows and necessities,
         for a mind to care for my fellow-men,
         for opportunities of spreading happiness around,
         for loved ones in the joys of heaven,
         for my own expectation of seeing thee clearly.
I love thee above the powers of language to express,
   for what thou art to thy creatures.

Increase my love, O my God, through time and eternity.

THE GIFT OF GIFTS

O SOURCE OF ALL GOOD,
What shall I render to thee for the gift of gifts,
   thine own dear Son, begotten, not created,
   my redeemer, proxy, surety, substitute,
   his self-emptying incomprehensible,
   his infinity of love beyond the heart's grasp.
Herein is wonder of wonders:
   he came below to raise me above,
   was born like me that I might become like him.
Herein is love;
   when I cannot rise to him he draws near on wings of grace,
      to raise me to himself.
Herein is power;
   when Deity and humanity were infinitely apart
   he united them in indissoluble unity, the uncreate and the created.
Herein is wisdom;
   when I was undone, with no will to return to him,
      and no intellect to devise recovery,
   he came, God-incarnate, to save me to the uttermost,
      as man to die my death,
         to shed satisfying blood on my behalf,
         to work out a perfect righteousness for me.
O God, take me in spirit to the watchful shepherds, and
   enlarge my mind;
   let me hear good tidings of great joy,
      and hearing, believe, rejoice, praise, adore,
      my conscience bathed in an ocean of repose,
      my eyes uplifted to a reconciled Father;
   place me with ox, ass, camel, goat,
      to look with them upon my redeemer's face,
      and in him account myself delivered from sin;
   let me with Simeon clasp the new-born child to my heart,
      embrace him with undying faith,
      exulting that he is mine and I am his.
In him thou hast given me so much that heaven can give no more.

CHRIST THE WORD

MY FATHER,
In a world of created changeable things,
    Christ and his Word alone remain unshaken.
O to forsake all creatures,
    to rest as a stone on him the foundation,
    to abide in him, be borne up by him!
For all my mercies come through Christ,
        who has designed, purchased, promised, effected them.
How sweet it is to be near him, the Lamb,
    filled with holy affections!
When I sin against thee I cross thy will, love, life,
    and have no comforter, no creature, to go to.
My sin is not so much this or that particular evil,
        but my continual separation, disunion, distance from thee,
    and having a loose spirit towards thee.
But thou hast given me a present, Jesus thy Son,
    as mediator between thyself and my soul,
    as middle-man who in a pit
        holds both him below and him above,
    for only he can span the chasm breached by sin,
        and satisfy divine justice.
May I always lay hold upon this mediator,
        as a realized object of faith,
        and alone worthy by his love to bridge the gulf.
Let me know that he is dear to me by his Word;
I am one with him by the Word on his part,
    and by faith on mine;
If I oppose the Word I oppose my Lord when he is most near;
If I receive the Word I receive my Lord wherein he is nigh.
O thou who hast the hearts of all men in thine hand,
        form my heart according to the Word,
                according to the image of thy Son,
So shall Christ the Word, and his Word, be my strength and comfort.

CHRIST IS ALL

O LOVER TO THE UTTERMOST,
    May I read the meltings of thy heart to me
        in the manger of thy birth,
        in the garden of thy agony,
        in the cross of thy suffering,
        in the tomb of thy resurrection,
        in the heaven of thy intercession.
    Bold in this thought I defy my adversary,
                tread down his temptations,
                resist his schemings,
                renounce the world,
                am valiant for truth.
Deepen in me a sense of my holy relationship to thee,
        as spiritual bridegroom,
        as Jehovah's fellow,
        as sinners' friend.
    I think of thy glory and my vileness,
        thy majesty and my meanness,
        thy beauty and my deformity,
        thy purity and my filth,
        thy righteousness and my iniquity.
Thou hast loved me everlastingly, unchangeably,
        may I love thee as I am loved;
Thou hast given thyself for me,
        may I give myself to thee;
Thou hast died for me,
        may I live to thee,
          in every moment of my time,
          in every movement of my mind,
          in every pulse of my heart.
May I never dally with the world and its allurements,
        but walk by thy side,
          listen to thy voice,
          be clothed with thy graces,
          and adorned with thy righteousness.

FULLNESS IN CHRIST

O GOD,
Thou hast taught me
    that Christ has all fullness and so all plenitude of the Spirit,
    that all fullness I lack in myself is in him,
      for his people, not for himself alone,
      he having perfect knowledge, grace, righteousness,
        to make me see,
        to make me righteous,
        to give me fullness;
    that it is my duty, out of a sense of emptiness,
      to go to Christ, possess, enjoy his fullness as mine,
      as if I had it in myself, because it is for me in him;
    that when I do this I am full of the Spirit,
      as a fish that has got from the shore to the sea
        and has all fullness of waters to move in,
      for when faith fills me, then I am full;
    that this is the way to be filled with the Spirit,
      like Stephen, first faith, then fullness,
      for this way makes me most empty,
      and so most fit for the Spirit to fill.
Thou hast taught me that
    the finding of this treasure of all grace in the field of Christ
      begets strength, joy, glory,
      and renders all graces alive.
Help me to delight more in what I receive from Christ,
          more in that fullness which is in him,
           the fountain of all his glory.
Let me not think to receive the Spirit from him as a 'thing'
    apart from finding, drinking, being filled with him.
To this end, O God,
    do thou establish me in Christ,
    settle me, give me a being there,
    assure me with certainty that all this is mine,
    for this only will fill my heart with joy and peace.

UNION WITH CHRIST

O FATHER.

Thou hast made man for the glory of thyself,
    and when not an instrument of that glory,
    he is a thing of nought;
No sin is greater than the sin of unbelief,
    for if union with Christ is the greatest good,
    unbelief is the greatest sin,
    as being cross to thy command;
I see that whatever my sin is,
    yet no sin is like disunion from Christ by unbelief.
Lord, keep me from committing the greatest sin in departing from him,
    for I can never in this life perfectly obey and cleave to Christ.
When thou takest away my outward blessings, it is for sin,
    in not acknowledging that all that I have is of thee,
    in not serving thee through what I have,
    in making myself secure and hardened.
Lawful blessings are the secret idols, and do most hurt;
    the greatest injury is in the having,
    the greatest good in the taking away.
In love divest me of blessings that I may glorify thee the more;
    remove the fuel of my sin,
    and may I prize the gain of a little holiness
    as overbalancing all my losses.
The more I love thee with a truly gracious love
    the more I desire to love thee,
    and the more miserable I am at my want of love;
The more I hunger and thirst after thee,
    the more I faint and fail in finding thee,
The more my heart is broken for sin,
    the more I pray it may be far more broken.

My great evil is that I do not remember the sins of my youth,
    nay, the sins of one day I forget the next.
Keep me from all things that turn to unbelief
    or lack of felt union with Christ.

THE NAME OF JESUS

ALL-SEARCHING GOD,
Thou readest the heart,
  viewest principles and motives of actions,
  seest more defilement in my duties
   than I ever saw in any of my sins.
The heavens are not clean in thy sight,
  and thou chargest the angels with folly;
I am ready to flee from myself because of my abominations;
Yet thou dost not abhor me
 but hast devised means for my return to thee,
 and that, by thy Son who died to give me life.

Thine honour is secured and displayed even in my escape from
 thy threats,
  and that, by means of Jesus
   in whom mercy and truth meet together,
   and righteousness and peace kiss each other.

In him the enslaved find redemption,
  the guilty pardon,
  the unholy renovation;
In him are everlasting strength for the weak,
   unsearchable riches for the needy,
    treasures of wisdom and knowledge for the ignorant,
    fullness for the empty.
At thy gracious call I hear, take, come, apply, receive his grace,
 not only submit to his mercy but acquiesce in it,
 not only glory in the cross but in him crucified and slain,
 not only joy in forgiveness but in the one through whom
  atonement comes.

Thy blessings are as secure as they are glorious;
Thou hast provided for my safety and my prosperity,
 and hast promised that I shall stand firm and grow stronger.
O Lord God, without the pardon of my sin I cannot rest satisfied.

without the renovation of my nature by grace I can never
    rest easy,
without the hopes of heaven I can never be at peace.
All this I have in thy Son Jesus; blessed be his name.

CHRIST ALONE

O GOD,
Thy main plan, and the end of thy will
    is to make Christ glorious and beloved in heaven
        where he is now ascended,
          where one day all the elect will behold his glory
          and love and glorify him for ever.
Though here I love him but little,
    may this be my portion at last.
In this world thou hast given me a beginning,
    one day it will be perfected in the realm above.
Thou hast helped me to see and know Christ, though obscurely,
    to take him, receive him,
    to possess him, love him,
    to bless him in my heart, mouth, life.
Let me study and stand for discipline,
    and all the ways of worship,
        out of love for Christ;
        and to show my thankfulness;
    to seek and know his will from love,
    to hold it in love,
    and daily to care for and keep this state of heart.
thou hast led me to place all my nature and happiness
    in oneness with Christ,
    in having heart and mind centred only on him,
    in being like him in communicating good to others;
This is my heaven on earth,
But I need the force, energy, impulses of thy Spirit
    to carry me on the way to my Jerusalem.
Here, it is my duty
    to be as Christ in this world,
    to do what he would do,
    to live as he would live,
    to walk in love and meekness;
    then would he be known,
    then would I have peace in death.

JESUS MY GLORY

O LORD GOD,
Thou hast commanded me to believe in Jesus;
 and I would flee to no other refuge,
   wash in no other fountain,
   build on no other foundation,
   receive from no other fullness,
   rest in no other relief.
His water and blood were not severed in their flow at the cross,
 may they never be separated in my creed and experiences;
May I be equally convinced of the guilt and pollution of sin,
 feel my need of a prince and saviour,
 implore of him repentance as well as forgiveness,
 love holiness, and be pure in heart,
 have the mind of Jesus, and tread in his steps.
Let me not be at my own disposal,
 but rejoice that I am under the care of one
 who is too wise to err,
  too kind to injure,
  too tender to crush.
May I scandalize none by my temper and conduct, but
 recommend and endear Christ to all around,
 bestow good on every one as circumstances permit,
 and decline no opportunity of usefulness.
Grant that I may value my substance,
 not as the medium of pride and luxury,
 but as the means of my support and stewardship.
Help me to guide my affections with discretion,
 to owe no man anything,
 to be able to give to him that needeth,
 to feel it my duty and pleasure to be merciful and forgiving,
 to show to the world the likeness of Jesus.

THE LOVE OF JESUS

O FATHER OF JESUS,

Help me to approach thee with deepest reverence, not with
   presumption,
      not with servile fear, but with holy boldness.
Thou art beyond the grasp of my understanding,
      but not beyond that of my love,
Thou knowest that I love thee supremely,
      for thou art supremely adorable, good, perfect.

My heart melts at the love of Jesus,
      my brother, bone of my bone, flesh of my flesh,
      married to me, dead for me, risen for me;
He is mine and I am his,
      given to me as well as for me;
I am never so much mine as when I am his,
      or so much lost to myself until lost in him;
      then I find my true manhood.

But my love is frost and cold, ice and snow;
Let his love warm me,
            lighten my burden,
            be my heaven;
May it be more revealed to me in all its influences
      that my love to him may be more fervent and glowing;
Let the mighty tide of his everlasting love
      cover the rocks of my sin and care;
Then let my spirit float above those things
      which had else wrecked my life.

Make me fruitful by living to that love,
      my character becoming more beautiful every day.
If traces of Christ's love-artistry be upon me,
      may he work on with his divine brush
      until the complete image be obtained
      and I be made a perfect copy of him, my master.

O Lord Jesus, come to me,
O Divine Spirit, rest upon me,
O Holy Father, look on me in mercy for the sake of the well-beloved.

[25]

LOVE TO JESUS

LORD JESUS,
If I love thee my soul shall seek thee,
    but can I seek thee unless my love to thee is kept
    alive to this end?
Do I love thee because thou art good,
    and canst alone do me good?
It is fitting thou shouldest not regard me,
    for I am vile and selfish;
    yet I seek thee,
    and when I find thee there is no wrath to devour me,
    but only sweet love.
Thou dost stand as a rock between the scorching sun and my soul,
    and I live under the cool lee-side as one elect.
When my mind acts without thee
    it spins nothing but deceit and delusion;
When my affections act without thee
    nothing is seen but dead works.
O how I need thee to abide in me,
    for I have no natural eyes to see thee,
    but I live by faith in one whose face to me
    is brighter than a thousand suns!
When I see that all sin is in me, all shame belongs to me;
    let me know that all good is in thee, all glory is thine.
Keep me from the error of thinking thou dost appear gloriously
    when some strange light fills my heart,
    as if that were the glorious activity of grace,
    but let me see that the truest revelation of thyself
    is when thou dost eclipse all my personal glory
    and all the honour, pleasure, and good of this world.
The Son breaks out in glory
    when he shows himself as one who outshines all creation,
    makes men poor in spirit,
    and helps them to find their good in him.
Grant that I may distrust myself, to see my all in thee.

THE SECOND COMING

O SON OF GOD AND SON OF MAN,
Thou wast incarnate, didst suffer, rise, ascend for my sake;
Thy departure was not a token of separation but a pledge of return;
Thy Word, promises, sacraments, show thy death until thou come
    again.
That day is no horror to me,
    for thy death has redeemed me,
        thy Spirit fills me,
        thy love animates me,
        thy Word governs me.
I have trusted thee and thou hast not betrayed my trust;
    waited for thee, and not waited in vain.
Thou wilt come to raise my body from the dust, and re-unite it to
    my soul,
    by a wonderful work of infinite power and love,
    greater than that which bounds the oceans' waters,
            ebbs and flows the tides,
            keeps the stars in their courses,
            and gives life to all creatures.
This corruptible shall put on incorruption,
    this mortal, immortality,
    this natural body, a spiritual body,
    this dishonoured body, a glorious body,
    this weak body, a body of power.
I triumph now in thy promises as I shall do in their performance,
    for the head cannot live if the members are dead;
Beyond the grave is resurrection, judgment, acquittal, dominion.
Every event and circumstance of my life will be dealt with—
    the sins of my youth, my secret sins,
    the sins of abusing thee, of disobeying thy Word,
    the sins of neglecting ministers' admonitions,
    the sins of violating my conscience—
        all will be judged;
And after judgment, peace and rest, life and service,
            employment and enjoyment, for thine elect.
O God, keep me in this faith, and ever looking for Christ's return.

SPIRITUS SANCTUS

O HOLY SPIRIT,
As the sun is full of light, the ocean full of water,
   Heaven full of glory, so may my heart be full of thee.
Vain are all divine purposes of love
   and the redemption wrought by Jesus
   except thou work within,
                  regenerating by thy power,
                  giving me eyes to see Jesus,
                  showing me the realities of the unseen world.
Give me thyself without measure,
   as an unimpaired fountain,
   as inexhaustible riches.
I bewail my coldness, poverty, emptiness,
               imperfect vision, languid service,
               prayerless prayers, praiseless praises.
Suffer me not to grieve or resist thee.
Come as power,
   to expel every rebel lust, to reign supreme and keep me thine;
Come as teacher,
   leading me into all truth, filling me with all understanding;
Come as love,
   that I may adore the Father, and love him as my all;
Come as joy,
   to dwell in me, move in me, animate me;
Come as light,
   illuminating the Scripture, moulding me in its laws;
Come as sanctifier,
   body, soul and spirit wholly thine;
Come as helper,
   with strength to bless and keep, directing my every step;
Come as beautifier,
   bringing order out of confusion, loveliness out of chaos.
Magnify to me thy glory by being magnified in me,
   and make me redolent of thy fragrance.

GOD THE SPIRIT

O LORD GOD,
I pray not so much for graces as for the Spirit himself,
    because I feel his absence,
    and act by my own spirit in everything.
Give me not weak desires but the power of his presence,
    for this is the surest way to have all his graces,
    and when I have the seal I have the impression also;
He can heal, help, quicken, humble suddenly and easily,
    can work grace and life effectually,
    and being eternal he can give grace eternally.
Save me from great hindrances,
    from being content with a little measure of the Spirit,
    from thinking thou wilt not give me more.
When I feel my lack of him, light up life and faith,
    for when I lose thee I am either in the dark and cannot see thee,
    or Satan and my natural abilities content me with a little light,
    so that I seek no further for the Spirit of life.
Teach me then what to do.
Should I merely humble myself and not stir up my heart?
Should I meditate and use all means to bring him near,
    not being contented by one means,
    but trust him to give me a blessing by the use of all,
    depending only upon, and waiting always for, thy light, by use
        of means?
Is it a duty or an error to pray
    and look for the fullness of the Spirit in me?
Am I mistaken in feeling I am empty of the Spirit
    because I do not sense his presence within,
    when all the time I am most empty
    and could be more full by faith in Christ?
Was the fullness of the Spirit in the apostles
    chiefly a power,
    giving them subsistence outside themselves in Christ,
    in whom was their life and joy?

Teach me to find and know fullness of the Spirit only in Jesus.

THE SPIRIT OF JESUS

LORD JESUS CHRIST,
Fill me with thy Spirit
    that I may be occupied with his presence.
I am blind – send him to make me see;
   dark – let him say, 'Let there be light'!
May he give me faith to behold
    my name engraven in thy hand,
    my soul and body redeemed by thy blood,
    my sinfulness covered by thy life of pure obedience.
Replenish me by his revealing grace,
    that I may realise my indissoluble union with thee;
    that I may know thou hast espoused me to thyself for ever,
      in righteousness, love, mercy, faithfulness;
    that I am one with thee,
      as a branch with its stock, as a building with its foundation.
May his comforts cheer me in my sorrows,
   his strength sustain me in my trials,
   his blessings revive me in my weariness,
   his presence render me a fruitful tree of holiness,
   his might establish me in peace and joy,
   his incitements make me ceaseless in prayer,
   his animation kindle in me undying devotion.
Send him as the searcher of my heart,
    to show me more of my corruptions and helplessness,
    that I may flee to thee,
        cling to thee,
       rest on thee,
   as the beginning and end of my salvation.
May I never vex him by my indifference and waywardness,
      grieve him by my cold welcome,
     resist him by my hard rebellion.

Answer my prayers, O Lord, for thy great name's sake.

THE SPIRIT'S WORK

O GOD THE HOLY SPIRIT,
Thou who dost proceed from the Father and the Son,
    have mercy on me.
When thou didst first hover over chaos, order came to birth,
    beauty robed the world, fruitfulness sprang forth.
Move, I pray thee, upon my disordered heart;
Take away the infirmities of unruly desires and hateful lusts;
Lift the mists and darkness of unbelief;
Brighten my soul with the pure light of truth;
Make it fragrant as the garden of paradise,
      rich with every goodly fruit,
      beautiful with heavenly grace,
      radiant with rays of divine light.
Fulfil in me the glory of thy divine offices;
Be my comforter, light, guide, sanctifier;
Take of the things of Christ and show them to my soul;
Through thee may I daily learn more of his love,
    grace, compassion, faithfulness, beauty;
Lead me to the cross and show me his wounds,
    the hateful nature of evil, the power of Satan;
May I there see my sins as the nails that transfixed him,
                the cords that bound him,
                the thorns that tore him,
                the sword that pierced him.
Help me to find in his death the reality and immensity of his love.
Open for me the wondrous volumes of truth in his, 'It is finished'.
Increase my faith in the clear knowledge of
    atonement achieved, expiation completed,
    satisfaction made, guilt done away,
    my debt paid, my sins forgiven,
    my person redeemed, my soul saved,
    hell vanquished, heaven opened, eternity made mine.
O Holy Spirit, deepen in me these saving lessons.
Write them upon my heart, that my walk be sin-loathing,
    sin-fleeing, Christ-loving;
And suffer no devil's device to beguile or deceive me.

THE SPIRIT AS TEACHER

O GOD THE HOLY SPIRIT,
That which I know not, teach thou me,
Keep me a humble disciple in the school of Christ,
    learning daily there what I am in myself,
        a fallen sinful creature,
    justly deserving everlasting destruction;
O let me never lose sight of my need of a saviour,
    or forget that apart from him I am nothing, and can do nothing.
Open my understanding to know the Holy Scriptures;
Reveal to my soul the counsels and works of the blessed Trinity;
Instil into my dark mind the saving knowledge of Jesus;
Make me acquainted with his covenant undertakings
    and his perfect fulfilment of them,
    that by resting on his finished work
    I may find the Father's love in the Son,
    his Father, my Father,
    and may be brought through thy influence
    to have fellowship with the Three in One.
O lead me into all truth, thou Spirit of wisdom and revelation,
    that I may know the things that belong unto my peace,
    and through thee be made anew.
Make practical upon my heart the Father's love
    as thou hast revealed it in the Scriptures;
Apply to my soul the blood of Christ, effectually, continually,
    and help me to believe, with conscience comforted,
    that it cleanseth from all sin;
Lead me from faith to faith,
    that I may at all times have freedom to come to a reconciled
      Father,
    and may be able to maintain peace with him
    against doubts, fears, corruptions, temptations.
Thy office is to teach me to draw near to Christ with a pure heart,
    steadfastly persuaded of his love,
    in the full assurance of faith.
Let me never falter in this way.

II

Redemption and Reconciliation

THE GOSPEL WAY

BLESSED LORD JESUS,
No human mind could conceive or invent the gospel.
Acting in eternal grace, thou art both its messenger and its message,
 lived out on earth through infinite compassion,
 applying thy life to insult, injury, death,
  that I might be redeemed, ransomed, freed.
Blessed be thou, O Father, for contriving this way,
Eternal thanks to thee, O Lamb of God, for opening this way,
Praise everlasting to thee, O Holy Spirit,
 for applying this way to my heart.
Glorious Trinity, impress the gospel on my soul,
 until its virtue diffuses every faculty;
Let it be heard, acknowledged, professed, felt.
Teach me to secure this mighty blessing;
Help me to give up every darling lust,
  to submit heart and life to its command,
  to have it in my will,
   controlling my affections,
   moulding my understanding;
  to adhere strictly to the rules of true religion,
   not departing from them in any instance,
   nor for any advantage in order to escape evil,
   inconvenience or danger.
Take me to the cross to seek glory from its infamy;
 Strip me of every pleasing pretence of righteousness by my own
 doings.
O gracious redeemer,
 I have neglected thee too long,
  often crucified thee,
  crucified thee afresh by my impenitence,
  put thee to open shame.
I thank thee for the patience that has borne with me so long,
 and for the grace that now makes me willing to be thine.
O unite me to thyself with inseparable bonds,
 that nothing may ever draw me back from thee, my Lord, my
 Saviour.

THE AWAKENED SINNER

O MY FORGETFUL SOUL,
Awake from thy wandering dream;
    turn from chasing vanities,
    look inward, forward, upward,
    view thyself,
    reflect upon thyself,
        who and what thou art, why here,
        what thou must soon be.
Thou art a creature of God,
    formed and furnished by him,
    lodged in a body like a shepherd in his tent;
    dost thou not desire to know God's ways?

O GOD,
Thou injured, neglected, provoked benefactor,
    when I think upon thy greatness and thy goodness
        I am ashamed at my insensibility,
        I blush to lift up my face,
        for I have foolishly erred.
Shall I go on neglecting thee,
    when every one of thy rational creatures should love thee,
    and take every care to please thee?
I confess that thou hast not been in all my thoughts,
        that the knowledge of thyself as the end of my being
            has been strangely overlooked,
        that I have never seriously considered my heart-need.
But although my mind is perplexed and divided, my nature perverse,
    yet my secret dispositions still desire thee.
Let me not delay to come to thee;
Break the fatal enchantment that binds my evil affections,
    and bring me to a happy mind that rests in thee,
    for thou hast made me and canst not forget me.
Let thy Spirit teach me the vital lessons of Christ,
    for I am slow to learn;
And hear thou my broken cries.

THE CONVICTING SPIRIT

THOU BLESSED SPIRIT, AUTHOR OF ALL GRACE AND COMFORT,
Come, work repentance in my soul;
Represent sin to me in its odious colours that I may hate it;
Melt my heart by the majesty and mercy of God;
Show me my ruined self and the help there is in him;
Teach me to behold my creator,
     his ability to save,
     his arms outstretched,
     his heart big for me.
May I confide in his power and love,
  commit my soul to him without reserve,
  bear his image, observe his laws, pursue his service,
  and be through time and eternity
   a monument to the efficacy of his grace,
   a trophy of his victory.
Make me willing to be saved in his way,
 perceiving nothing in myself, but all in Jesus:
Help me not only to receive him but
    to walk in him,
    depend upon him,
    commune with him,
    be conformed to him,
    follow him,
     imperfect, but still pressing forward,
     not complaining of labour, but valuing rest,
     not murmuring under trials, but thankful for my state.
Give me that faith which is the means of salvation,
 and the principle and medium of all godliness;
May I be saved by grace through faith,
  live by faith,
  feel the joy of faith,
  do the work of faith.
Perceiving nothing in myself, may I find in Christ
  wisdom, righteousness, sanctification, redemption.

THE CRY OF A CONVICTED SINNER

THOU RIGHTEOUS AND HOLY SOVEREIGN,
In whose hand is my life and whose are all my ways,
Keep me from fluttering about religion;
    fix me firm in it,
    for I am irresolute;
    my decisions are smoke and vapour,
    and I do not glorify thee,
    or behave according to thy will;
Cut me not off before my thoughts grow to responses,
    and the budding of my soul into full flower,
    for thou art forbearing and good,
    patient and kind.
Save me from myself,
    from the artifices and deceits of sin,
    from the treachery of my perverse nature,
    from denying thy charge against my offences,
    from a life of continual rebellion against thee,
    from wrong principles, views, and ends;
    for I know that all my thoughts, affections,
        desires and pursuits are alienated from thee.
I have acted as if I hated thee, although thou art love itself;
 have contrived to tempt thee to the uttermost,
    to wear out thy patience;
 have lived evilly in word and action.
Had I been a prince
  I would long ago have crushed such a rebel;
Had I been a father
  I would long since have rejected my child.
O, thou Father of my spirit,
 thou king of my life,
     cast me not into destruction,
     drive me not from thy presence,
     but wound my heart that it may be healed;
     break it that thine own hand may make it whole.

GOD AND MYSELF

LORD GOD ALMIGHTY,
Thy understanding is unsearchable and infinite,
Thy arm cannot be stayed,
Thy agency extends through limitless space,
All works hang on thy care,
With thee time is a present *now*.

Holy is thy wisdom, power, mercy, ways, works.
How can I stand before thee
    with my numberless and aggravated offences?
I have often loved darkness,
        observed lying vanities,
        forsaken thy given mercies,
        trampled underfoot thy beloved Son,
        mocked thy providences,
        flattered thee with my lips,
        broken thy covenant.
It is of thy compassion that I am not consumed.

Lead me to repentance, and save me from despair;
Let me come to thee renouncing, condemning, loathing myself,
    but hoping in the grace that flows even to the chief of sinners.
At the cross may I contemplate the evil of sin, and abhor it,
        look on him whom I pierced,
          as one slain for me, and by me.
May I never despise his death by fearing its efficacy for my salvation.
And whatever cross I am required to bear,
    let me see him carrying a heavier.
Teach me in health to think of sickness,
        in the brightest hours to be ready for darkness;
        in life prepare me for death.
Thus may my soul rest in thee, O immortal and transcendent one,
    revealed as thou art in the Person and work of thy Son,
    the friend of sinners.

THE MEDIATOR

EVERLASTING CREATOR–FATHER,
I have destroyed myself,
 my nature is defiled,
 the powers of my soul are degraded;
 I am vile, miserable, strengthless,
 but my hope is in thee.
If ever I am saved it will be by goodness undeserved and astonishing,
 not by mercy alone but by abundant mercy,
 not by grace but by exceeding riches of grace;
And such thou hast revealed, promised, exemplified
 in thoughts of peace, not of evil.

Thou hast devised means
 to rescue me from sin's perdition,
 to restore me to happiness, honour, safety.
I bless thee for the everlasting covenant,
  for the appointment of a mediator.
I rejoice that he failed not, nor was discouraged,
 but accomplished the work thou gavest him to do;
 and said on the cross, 'It is finished.'
I exult in the thought that
 thy justice is satisfied,
 thy truth established,
 thy law magnified,
  and a foundation is laid for my hope.
I look to a present and personal interest in Christ and say,
 Surely he has borne my griefs, carried my sorrows,
  won my peace, healed my soul.
Justified by his blood I am saved by his life,
Glorying in his cross I bow to his sceptre,
Having his Spirit I possess his mind.

Lord, grant that my religion may not be occasional and partial,
 but universal, influential, effective,
 and may I always continue in thy words as well as thy works,
 so that I may reach my end in peace.

THE PRECIOUS BLOOD

BLESSED LORD JESUS,
Before thy cross I kneel and see
      the heinousness of my sin,
      my iniquity that caused thee to be 'made a curse',
      the evil that excites the severity of divine wrath.
Show me the enormity of my guilt by
      the crown of thorns,
      the pierced hands and feet,
      the bruised body,
      the dying cries.
Thy blood is the blood of incarnate God,
      its worth infinite, its value beyond all thought.
Infinite must be the evil and guilt that demands such a price.
Sin is my malady, my monster, my foe, my viper,
    born in my birth,
    alive in my life,
    strong in my character,
    dominating my faculties,
    following me as a shadow,
    intermingling with my every thought,
    my chain that holds me captive in the empire of my soul.
    Sinner that I am, why should the sun give me light,
            the air supply breath,
            the earth bear my tread,
            its fruits nourish me,
            its creatures subserve my ends?
Yet thy compassions yearn over me,
    thy heart hastens to my rescue,
    thy love endured my curse,
    thy mercy bore my deserved stripes.
Let me walk humbly in the lowest depths of humiliation,
      bathed in thy blood,
      tender of conscience,
      triumphing gloriously as an heir of salvation.

LOVE LUSTRES AT CALVARY

MY FATHER,
Enlarge my heart, warm my affections, open my lips,
    supply words that proclaim 'Love lustres at Calvary.'
There grace removes my burdens and heaps them on thy Son,
    made a transgressor, a curse, and sin for me;
There the sword of thy justice smote the man, thy fellow;
There thy infinite attributes were magnified,
    and infinite atonement was made;
There infinite punishment was due,
    and infinite punishment was endured.
Christ was all anguish that I might be all joy,
        cast off that I might be brought in,
        trodden down as an enemy
           that I might be welcomed as a friend,
        surrendered to hell's worst
           that I might attain heaven's best,
        stripped that I might be clothed,
        wounded that I might be healed,
        athirst that I might drink,
        tormented that I might be comforted,
        made a shame that I might inherit glory.
        entered darkness that I might have eternal light,
My Saviour wept that all tears might be wiped from my eyes,
        groaned that I might have endless song,
        endured all pain that I might have unfading health,
        bore a thornèd crown that I might have a glory-diadem,
        bowed his head that I might uplift mine,
        experienced reproach that I might receive welcome,
        closed his eyes in death that I might gaze on unclouded
           brightness,
        expired that I might for ever live.
O Father, who spared not thine only Son that thou mightest spare me,
All this transfer thy love designed and accomplished;
Help me to adore thee by lips and life.
O that my every breath might be ecstatic praise,
    my every step buoyant with delight, as I see

my enemies crushed,
　　Satan baffled, defeated, destroyed,
　　sin buried in the ocean of reconciling blood,
　　　hell's gates closed, heaven's portal open.
Go forth, O conquering God, and show me the cross,
　　mighty to subdue, comfort and save.

THE SAVIOUR

THOU GOD OF ALL GRACE,
 Thou hast given me a saviour,
 produce in me a faith to live by him,
      to make him all my desire,
        all my hope,
        all my glory.
 May I enter him as my refuge,
  build on him as my foundation,
  walk in him as my way,
  follow him as my guide,
  conform to him as my example,
  receive his instructions as my prophet,
  rely on his intercession as my high priest,
  obey him as my king.
May I never be ashamed of him or his words,
  but joyfully bear his reproach,
  never displease him by unholy or imprudent conduct,
  never count it a glory if I take it patiently
   when buffeted for a fault,
  never make the multitude my model,
  never delay when thy Word invites me to advance.
May thy dear Son preserve me from this present evil world,
  so that its smiles never allure,
  nor its frowns terrify,
  nor its vices defile,
  nor its errors delude me.
May I feel that I am a stranger and a pilgrim on earth,
    declaring plainly that I seek a country,
    my title to it becoming daily more clear,
    my meetness for it more perfect,
    my foretastes of it more abundant;
and whatsoever I do may it be done in the Saviour's name.

RECONCILIATION

LORD GOD ALMIGHTY,
Thou art beforehand with men
    for thou hast reconciled thyself to the world through the cross,
    and dost beseech men to accept reconciliation.
It is my responsibility to grasp thy overtures of grace,
    for if thou, the offended party, act first
        with the word of appeasement,
    I need not call in question thy willingness to save,
    but must deplore my own foolish maliciousness;
If I do not come to thee as one who seeks thy favour,
    I live in contempt, anger, malice, self-sufficiency,
    and thou dost call it enmity.
Thou hast taught me the necessity of a mediator, a messiah,
    to be embraced in love with all my heart,
        as king to rule me,
        as prophet to guide me,
        as priest to take away my sin and death,
    and this by faith in thy beloved Son who teaches me
        not to guide myself,
        not to obey myself,
        not to try to rule and conquer sin,
        but to cleave to the one who will do all for me.
Thou hast made known to me
    that to save me is Christ's work,
        but to cleave to him by faith is my work,
    and with this faith is the necessity of my daily repentance
        as a mourning for the sin which Christ by grace has removed.
Continue, O God, to teach me
    that faith apprehends Christ's righteousness
        not only for the satisfaction of justice,
        but as unspotted evidence of thy love to me.
Help me to make use of his work of salvation as the ground of peace,
    and of thy favour to, and acceptance of me the sinner,
    so that I may live always near the cross.

DELIVERANCE

O GOD OF UNSEARCHABLE GREATNESS,
Before thee I am nothing but vanity, iniquity, perishing;
Sin has forfeited thy favour,
>stripped me of thy image,
>banished me from thy presence,
>exposed me to the curse of thy law;

I cannot deliver myself, and am in despair.
But a resource is found in thee,
>for without my desert or desire
>thou didst devise an everlasting plan,
>honourable to thy perfections,
>and which angels desired to look into.
And the Word which announces all the glory of this goodness
>is nigh me, invites me, beseeches me.
May I, a convinced and self-despairing sinner.
>find Jesus as the power unto salvation,
>his death the centre of all relief,
>>the source of all gospel-blessings.
Help me to repair to that cross,
>be crucified to the world by it,
>and in it find deepest humiliation,
>>motives to patience and self-denial,
>>grace for active benevolence,
>>faith to grasp eternal life,
>>hope to lift up my head,
>>love to bind me for ever
>>to him who died and rose for me.
May his shed blood make me
>more thankful for thy mercies,
>more humble under thy correction,
>more zealous in thy service,
>more watchful against temptation,
>more contented in my circumstances,
>more useful to others.

REGENERATION

O GOD OF THE HIGHEST HEAVEN,
    occupy the throne of my heart,
    take full possession and reign supreme,
    lay low every rebel lust,
    let no vile passion resist thy holy war;
    manifest thy mighty power,
       and make me thine for ever.
Thou art worthy to be praised with my every breath,
          loved with my every faculty of soul,
          served with my every act of life.
Thou hast loved me, espoused me, received me,
      purchased, washed, favoured, clothed, adorned me,
        when I was worthless, vile, soiled, polluted.
I was dead in iniquities,
    having no eyes to see thee,
       no ears to hear thee,
       no taste to relish thy joys,
       no intelligence to know thee;
But thy Spirit has quickened me,
       has brought me into a new world as a new creature,
       has given me spiritual perception,
       has opened to me thy Word as light, guide, solace, joy.
Thy presence is to me a treasure of unending peace;
No provocation can part me from thy sympathy,
    for thou hast drawn me with cords of love,
    and dost forgive me daily, hourly.
O help me then to walk worthy of thy love,
    of my hopes, and my vocation.
Keep me, for I cannot keep myself;
Protect me that no evil befall me;
Let me lay aside every sin admired of many;
Help me to walk by thy side, lean on thy arm,
    hold converse with thee,
That henceforth I may be salt of the earth and a blessing to all.

RESURRECTION

O GOD OF MY EXODUS,
Great was the joy of Israel's sons
  when Egypt died upon the shore,
Far greater the joy
  when the redeemer's foe lay crushed in the dust.
Jesus strides forth as the victor,
  conqueror of death, hell, and all opposing might;
He bursts the bands of death,
  tramples the powers of darkness down,
  and lives for ever.
He, my gracious surety,
  apprehended for payment of my debt,
  comes forth from the prison house of the grave
  free, and triumphant over sin, Satan, and death.
Show me herein the proof that his vicarious offering is accepted,
  that the claims of justice are satisfied,
  that the devil's sceptre is shivered,
  that his wrongful throne is levelled.
Give me the assurance that in Christ I died, in him I rose,
    in his life I live, in his victory I triumph,
    in his ascension I shall be glorified.
Adorable redeemer,
  thou who wast lifted up upon a cross
  art ascended to highest heaven.
Thou, who as man of sorrows wast crowned with thorns,
  art now as Lord of life wreathed with glory.
Once, no shame more deep than thine,
  no agony more bitter, no death more cruel.
Now, no exaltation more high,
  no life more glorious, no advocate more effective.
Thou art in the triumph car leading captive thine enemies behind thee.
What more could be done than thou hast done!
  Thy death is my life, thy resurrection my peace,
  thy ascension my hope, thy prayers my comfort.

ELECTION

HOLY TRINITY,
All praise to thee for electing me to salvation,
    by foreknowledge of God the Father,
    through sanctification of the Spirit,
    unto obedience and sprinkling of the blood of Jesus;
I adore the wonders of thy condescending love,
  marvel at the true believer's high privilege
                within whom all heaven comes to dwell,
            abiding in God and God in him;
I believe it, help me experience it to the full.
Continue to teach me that Christ's righteousness
    satisfies justice and evidences thy love;
Help me to make use of it by faith as the ground of my peace
    and of thy favour and acceptance,
    so that I may live always near the cross.
It is not feeling the Spirit that proves my saved state
    but the truth of what Christ did perfectly for me;
All holiness in him is by faith made mine,
    as if I had done it;
Therefore I see the use of his righteousness,
    for satisfaction to divine justice and making me righteous.
It is not inner sensation that makes Christ's death mine
    for that may be delusion, being without the Word,
    but his death apprehended by my faith,
    and so testified by Word and Spirit,
I bless thee for these lively exercises of faith,
    for the righteousness that is mine in Jesus,
    for grace to resign my will to thee;
I rejoice to think that all things are at thy disposal,
    and I love to leave them there.
Then prayer turns wholly into praise,
    and all I can do is to adore and love thee.
I want not the favour of man to lean upon,
    for I know that thy electing grace is infinitely better.

CHRISTIAN CALLING

O LORD GOD,
The first act of calling is by thy command in thy Word,
    'Come unto me, return unto me';
The second is to let in light,
    so that I see that I am called particularly,
    and perceive the sweetness of the command as well as its truth,
    in regard to thy great love of the sinner,
            by inviting him to come, though vile,
    in regard to the end of the command,
            which is fellowship with thee,
    in regard to thy promise in the gospel,
            which is all of grace.
Therefore, Lord,
    I need not search to see if I am elect, or loved,
            for if I turn thou wilt come to me;
    Christ has promised me fellowship if I take him,
    and the Spirit will pour himself out on me,
            abolishing sin and punishment,
            assuring me of strength to persevere.
It is thy pleasure to help all that pray for grace,
    and come to thee for it.
When my heart is unsavoury with sin, sorrow, darkness, hell,
    only thy free grace can help me act
    with deep abasement under a sense of unworthiness.
Let me lament for forgetting daily to come to thee,
    and cleanse me from the deceit of bringing my heart to a duty
    because the act pleased me or appealed to reason.
Grant that I may be salted with suffering,
    with every exactment tempered to my soul,
        every rod excellently fitted to my back,
        to chastise, humble, break me.
Let me not overlook the hand that holds the rod,
    as thou didst not let me forget the rod that fell on Christ,
    and drew me to him.

ASSURANCE

ALMIGHTY GOD,
I am loved with everlasting love,
    clothed in eternal righteousness,
        my peace flowing like a river,
        my comforts many and large,
        my joy and triumph unutterable,
        my soul lively with a knowledge of salvation,
        my sense of justification unclouded.
I have scarce anything to pray for;
Jesus smiles upon my soul as a ray of heaven
        and my supplications are swallowed up in praise.
How sweet is the glorious doctrine of election
        when based upon thy Word
        and wrought inwardly within the soul!
I bless thee that thou wilt keep the sinner thou hast loved,
        and hast engaged that he will not forsake thee,
        else I would never get to heaven.
I wrong the work of grace in my heart
        if I deny my new nature and my eternal life.
If Jesus were not my righteousness and redemption,
        I would sink into nethermost hell
        by my misdoings, shortcomings, unbelief, unlove;
If Jesus were not by the power of his Spirit my sanctification,
        there is no sin I should not commit.
O when shall I have his mind!
        when shall I be conformed to his image?
All the good things of life are less than nothing
        when compared with his love,
        and with one glimpse of thy electing favour.
All the treasures of a million worlds could not make me richer,
        happier, more contented,
        for his unsearchable riches are mine.
One moment of communion with him, one view of his grace,
        is ineffable, inestimable.
But O God, I could not long after thy presence
        if I did not know the sweetness of it;

And such I could not know except by thy Spirit in my heart,
    nor love thee at all unless thou didst
    elect me, call me, adopt me, save me.
I bless thee for the covenant of grace.

A CONVERT'S FIRST PRAYER

MY FATHER,
I could never have sought my happiness in thy love,
 unless thou had'st first loved me.
Thy Spirit has encouraged me by grace to seek thee,
  has made known to me thy reconciliation in Jesus,
  has taught me to believe it,
  has helped me to take thee for my God and portion.
May he grant me to grow in the knowledge and experience of thy love,
 and walk in it all the way to glory.
Blessed for ever be thy fatherly affection,
 which chose me to be one of thy children
 by faith in Jesus:
I thank thee for giving me the desire to live as such.
In Jesus, my brother, I have my new birth,
   every restraining power,
   every renewing grace.
It is by thy Spirit I call thee Father,
 believe in thee, love thee;
Strengthen me inwardly for every purpose of my Christian life;
Let the Spirit continually reveal to me my interest in Christ,
 and open to me the riches of thy love in him;
May he abide in me that I may know my union with Jesus,
 and enter into constant fellowship with him;
By the Spirit may I daily live to thee,
 rejoice in thy love,
 find it the same to me as to thy Son,
 and become rooted and grounded in it as a house on rock;
I know but little—
 increase my knowledge of thy love in Jesus,
 keep me pressing forward for clearer discoveries of it,
 so that I may find its eternal fullness;
Magnify thy love to me according to its greatness,
 and not according to my deserts or prayers,
 and whatever increase thou givest, let it draw out greater love
  to thee.

THE LIFE LOOK

O GOD,
I bless thee for the happy moment
    when I first saw thy law fulfilled in Christ,
      wrath appeased, death destroyed, sin forgiven, my soul saved.
Ever since, Thou hast been faithful to me,
    daily have I proved the power of Jesus' blood,
    daily have I known the strength of the Spirit,
      my teacher, director, sanctifier.
I want no other rock to build upon than that I have,
  desire no other hope than that of gospel truth,
  need no other look than that which gazes on the cross.
Forgive me if I have tried to add anything to the one foundation,
      if I have unconsciously relied upon my knowledge,
        experience, deeds, and not seen them as filthy rags,
      if I have attempted to complete what is perfect in Christ;
May my cry be always, Only Jesus! only Jesus!
In him is freedom from condemnation,
    fullness in his righteousness,
    eternal vitality in his given life,
    indissoluble union in fellowship with him;
In him I have all that I can hold;
    enlarge me to take in more.
If I backslide,
    let me like Peter weep bitterly and return to him;
If I am tempted, and have no wit,
    give me strength enough to trust in him;
If I am weak,
    may I faint upon his bosom of eternal love;
If in extremity,
    let me feel that he can deliver me;
If driven to the verge of hope and to the pit of despair,
    grant me grace to fall into his arms.
O God, hear me, do for me more than I ask, think, or dream.

VICTORY

O DIVINE REDEEMER,
Great was thy goodness
    in undertaking my redemption,
    in consenting to be made sin for me,
    in conquering all my foes;
    Great was thy strength
    in enduring the extremities of divine wrath,
    in taking away the load of my iniquities;
Great was thy love
    in manifesting thyself alive,
    in showing thy sacred wounds,
        that every fear might vanish, and every doubt be removed;
Great was thy mercy
    in ascending to heaven
    in being crowned and enthroned
        there to intercede for me,
        there to succour me in temptation,
        there to open the eternal book,
        there to receive me finally to thyself;
Great was thy wisdom
    in devising this means of salvation;
Bathe my soul in rich consolations of thy resurrection life;
Great was thy grace
    in commanding me to come hand in hand with thee to the Father,
        to be knit to him eternally,
        to discover in him my rest,
        to find in him my peace,
        to behold his glory,
        to honour him who is alone worthy;
    in giving me the Spirit as teacher, guide, power, that
        I may live repenting of sin,
        conquer Satan, find victory in life.
When thou art absent all sorrows are here,
When thou art present all blessings are mine.

FREEDOM

O HOLY FATHER, thou hast freely given thy Son,
O DIVINE SON, thou hast freely paid my debt,
O ETERNAL SPIRIT, thou dost freely bid me come,
O TRIUNE GOD, thou dost freely grace me with salvation.

Prayers and tears could not suffice to pardon my sins,
    nor anything less than atoning blood,
    but my believing is my receiving,
    for a thankful acceptance is no paying of the debt.
What didst thou see in me?
    that I a poor, diseased, despised sinner
      should be clothed in thy bright glory?
    that a creeping worm
      should be advanced to this high state?
    that one lately groaning, weeping, dying,
      should be as full of joy as my heart can hold?
    that a being of dust and darkness
      should be taken like Mordecai from captivity,
        and set next to the king?
      should be lifted like Daniel from a den
      and be made ruler of princes and provinces?
Who can fathom immeasurable love?
As far as the rational soul exceeds the senses,
    so does the spirit exceed the rational in its knowledge of thee.
Thou hast given me understanding to compass the earth,
    measure the sun, moon, stars, universe,
    but above all to know thee, the only true God.
I marvel that the finite can know the Infinite,
    here a little, afterwards in full-orbed truth;
Now I know but a small portion of what I shall know,
    here in part, there in perfection,
    here a glimpse, there a glory.
To enjoy thee is life eternal, and to enjoy is to know.
Keep me in the freedom of experiencing thy salvation continually.

BELONGING TO JESUS

O HEAVENLY FATHER,
Teach me to see
    that if Christ has pacified thee and satisfied divine justice
      he can also deliver me from my sins;
    that Christ does not desire me, now justified,
      to live in self-confidence in my own strength,
        but gives me the law of the Spirit of life
          to enable me to obey thee;
    that the Spirit and his power are mine
      by resting on Christ's death;
    that the Spirit of Life within answers to the law without;
    that if I sin not I should thank thee for it;
    that if I sin I should be humbled daily under it;
    that I should mourn for sin more than other men do,
      for when I see I shall die because of sin,
        that makes me mourn;
      when I see how sin strikes at thee,
        that makes me mourn;
      when I see that sin caused Christ's death,
    that makes me mourn;
    that sanctification is the evidence of reconciliation,
      proving that faith has truly apprehended Christ;
Thou hast taught me
    that faith is nothing else than receiving thy kindness;
    that it is an adherence to Christ, a resting on him,
      love clinging to him as a branch to the tree,
        to seek life and vigour from him.
I thank thee for showing me the vast difference
    between knowing things by reason,
    and knowing them by the spirit of faith.
By reason I see a thing is so; by faith I know it as it is.
I have seen thee by reason and have not been amazed,
I have seen thee as thou art in thy Son
    and have been ravished to behold thee.
I bless thee that I am thine in my Saviour, Jesus.

LIVING FOR JESUS

O SAVIOUR OF SINNERS,
Thy name is excellent,
   thy glory high,
   thy compassions unfailing,
   thy condescension wonderful,
   thy mercy tender.
I bless thee for the discoveries, invitations, promises of the gospel,
   for in them is pardon for rebels,
                  liberty for captives,
                  health for the sick,
                  salvation for the lost.
I come to thee in thy beloved name of Jesus;
   re-impress thy image upon my soul;
Raise me above the smiles and frowns of the world,
   regarding it as a light thing to be judged by men;
May thy approbation be my only aim,
      thy Word my one rule.
Make me to abhor that which grieves thy Holy Spirit,
         to suspect consolations of a worldly nature,
         to shun a careless way of life,
         to reprove evil,
         to instruct with meekness those who oppose me,
         to be gentle and patient towards all men,
         to be not only a professor but an example of the gospel,
            displaying in every relation, office, and condition
               its excellency, loveliness and advantages.
How little have I illustrated my principles
   and improved my privileges!
How seldom have I served my generation!
How often have I injured and not recommended my redeemer!
How few are those blessed through me!
In many things I have offended,
   in all come short of thy glory;
Pardon my iniquity, for it is great.

KEPT BY GOD

JEHOVAH GOD,
Thou creator, upholder, proprietor of all things,
I cannot escape from thy presence or control,
   nor do I desire to do so.
My privilege is to be under the agency of omnipotence,
   righteousness, wisdom, patience, mercy, grace.
Thou art love with more than parental affection;
I admire thy heart, adore thy wisdom,
   stand in awe of thy power, abase myself before thy purity.
It is the discovery of thy goodness alone that can
              banish my fear,
              allure me into thy presence,
              help me to bewail and confess my sins.
When I review my past guilt
   and am conscious of my present unworthiness
     I tremble to come to thee,
     I whose foundation is in the dust,
     I who have condemned thy goodness,
          defied thy power,
          trampled upon thy love,
          rendered myself worthy of eternal death.

But my recovery cannot spring from any cause in me,
   I can destroy but cannnot save myself.
Yet thou hast laid help on One that is mighty,
   for there is mercy with thee,
     and exceeding riches in thy kindness through Jesus.
May I always feel my need of him.
Let thy restored joy be my strength;
May it keep me from lusting after the world,
        bear up heart and mind in loss of comforts,
        enliven me in the valley of death,
        work in me the image of the heavenly,
        and give me to enjoy the first fruits of spirituality,
      such as angels and departed saints know.

A CHRISTIAN'S PRAYER

BLESSED GOD,
 Ten thousand snares are mine without and within,
  defend thou me;
 When sloth and indolence seize me,
  give me views of heaven;
 When sinners entice me,
  give me disrelish of their ways;
 When sensual pleasures tempt me,
  purify and refine me;
 When I desire worldly possessions,
  help me to be rich toward thee;
 When the vanities of the world ensnare me,
  let me not plunge into new guilt and ruin.
 May I remember the dignity of my spiritual release,
  never be too busy to attend to my soul,
  never be so engrossed with time
  that I neglect the things of eternity;
  thus may I not only live, but grow towards thee.
 Form my mind to right notions of religion,
  that I may not judge of grace by wrong conceptions,
  nor measure my spiritual advances
  by the efforts of my natural being.
 May I seek after an increase of divine love to thee,
    after unreserved resignation to thy will,
    after extensive benevolence to my fellow
     creatures,
    after patience and fortitude of soul,
    after a heavenly disposition
    after a concern that I may please thee in public
    and private.
 Draw on my soul the lineaments of Christ,
  in every trace and feature of which thou wilt take
   delight, for I am thy workmanship,
  created in Christ Jesus,
  thy letter written with the Holy Spirit's pen,
  thy tilled soil ready for the sowing, then harvest.

AMAZING GRACE

O THOU GIVING GOD,
My heart is drawn out in thankfulness to thee,
 for thy amazing grace and condescension to me
 in influences and assistances of thy Spirit,
 for special help in prayer,
 for the sweetness of Christian service,
 for the thoughts of arriving in heaven,
 for always sending me needful supplies,
 for raising me to new life when I am like one dead.
I want not the favour of man to lean upon
 for thy favour is infinitely better.
Thou art eternal wisdom in dispensations towards me;
 and it matters not when, nor where, nor how I serve thee,
 nor what trials I am exercised with,
 if I might but be prepared for thy work and will.
No poor creature stands in need of divine grace
 more than I do,
And yet none abuses it more than I have done, and still do.
How heartless and dull I am!
Humble me in the dust for not loving thee more.
Every time I exercise any grace renewedly
 I am renewedly indebted to thee,
 the God of all grace, for special assistance.
I cannot boast when I think how dependent I am upon thee
 for the being and every act of grace;
I never do anything else but depart from thee,
 and if ever I get to heaven it will be because thou willest it,
 and for no reason beside.
I love, as a feeble, afflicted, despised creature,
 to cast myself on thy infinite grace and goodness,
 hoping for no happiness but from thee;
Give me special grace to fit me for special services,
 and keep me calm and resigned at all times,
 humble, solemn, mortified, and conformed to thy will.

THE GREAT DISCOVERY

GLORIOUS GOD,
I bless thee that I know thee.
I once lived in the world, but was ignorant of its creator,
  was partaker of thy providences, but knew not the provider,
  was blind while enjoying the sunlight,
    was deaf to all things spiritual, with voices all around me,
  understood many things, but had no knowledge of thy ways,
  saw the world, but did not see Jesus only.
O happy day, when in thy love's sovereignty
  thou didst look on me, and call me by grace.
Then did the dead heart begin to beat,
      the darkened eye glimmer with light,
      the dull ear catch thy echo,
      and I turned to thee and found thee,
      a God ready to hear, willing to save.
Then did I find my heart at enmity to thee, vexing thy Spirit;
Then did I fall at thy feet and hear thee thunder,
  'The soul that sinneth, it must die',
But when grace made me to know thee,
  and admire a God who hated sin,
  thy terrible justice held my will submissive.
My thoughts were then as knives cutting my head.
Then didst thou come to me in silken robes of love,
  and I saw thy Son dying that I might live,
  and in that death I found my all.
My soul doth sing at the remembrance of that peace;
The gospel cornet brought a sound unknown to me before
        that reached my heart – and *I lived*—
          never to lose my hold on Christ or his hold on me.
Grant that I may always weep to the praise of mercy found,
  and tell to others as long as I live,
  that thou art a sin-pardoning God,
  taking up the blasphemer and the ungodly,
    and washing them from their deepest stain.

A NEOPHYTE'S DEVOTION

GLORIOUS AND HOLY GOD,
Provocations against thy divine majesty have filled my whole life,
   My offences have been countless and aggravated.
                 Conscience has rebuked me,
                 friends have admonished me,
                 the examples of others have reproached me,
                 thy rod has chastised me,
                 thy kindnesses allured me.
Thou hast seen and abhorred all my sins and
   couldst easily and justly have punished me,
      yet thou hast spared me,
            been gracious unto me,
            given me thy help,
            invited me to thy table.
Lord, I thankfully obey thy call,
      accept of thy goodness,
      acquiesce in thy gospel appointments.
I believe that Jesus thy Son has plenteous redemption;
I apply to him for his benefits,
  give up my mind implicitly to his instructions,
  trust and glory in his sacrifice,
  revere and love his authority,
  pray that his grace may reign in my life.
I will not love a world that crucified him,
   neither cherish nor endure the sin that put him to grief,
    nor suffer him to be wounded by others.
At the cross that relieves my conscience
   let me learn lessons of self-denial, forgiveness and submission,
      feel motives to obedience,
      find resources for all needs of the divine life.
Then let me *be* what I *profess*,
     do as well as *teach*,
     live as well as *hear* religion.

THE 'NEVERS' OF THE GOSPEL

O LORD,
May I
    never fail to come to the knowledge of the truth,
    never rest in a system of doctrine, however scriptural,
      that does not bring or further salvation,
        or teach me to deny ungodliness and worldly lusts,
        or help me to live soberly, righteously, godly;
    never rely on my own convictions and resolutions,
      but be strong in thee and in thy might;
    never cease to find thy grace sufficient
      in all my duties, trials, and conflicts;
    never forget to repair to thee
      in all my spiritual distresses and outward troubles,
      in all the dissatisfactions experienced in creature comforts;
    never fail to retreat to him who is full of grace and truth,
      the friend that loveth at all times,
      who is touched with feelings of my infirmities,
      and can do exceeding abundantly for me;
    never confine my religion to extraordinary occasions,
      but acknowledge thee in all my ways;
    never limit my devotions to particular seasons
      but be in thy fear all the day long;
    never be godly only on the sabbath or in thy house,
      but on every day abroad and at home;
    never make piety a dress but a habit,
      not only a habit but a nature,
      not only a nature but a life.
Do good to me by all thy dispensations,
          by all means of grace,
          by worship, prayers, praises,
And at last let me enter that world where is no temple,
    but only thy glory and the Lamb's.

TRUE RELIGION

LORD GOD ALMIGHTY,
I ask not to be enrolled amongst the earthly great and rich,
    but to be numbered with the spiritually blessed.
Make it my present, supreme, persevering concern
    to obtain those blessings which are
            spiritual in their nature,
            eternal in their continuance,
            satisfying in their possession.
Preserve me from a false estimate of the whole or a part of my
    character;
May I pay regard to my principles as well as my conduct,
                my motives as well as my actions.
Help me never to mistake the excitement of my passions
            for the renewing of the Holy Spirit,
            never to judge my religion by occasional impressions and
            impulses, but by my constant and prevailing disposition.
May my heart be right with thee, and my life as becometh the gospel.
May I maintain a supreme regard to another and better world,
    and feel and confess myself a stranger and a pilgrim here.
Afford me all the direction, defence, support, and consolation
    my journey hence requires,
    and grant me a mind stayed upon thee.
Give me large abundance of the supply of the Spirit of Jesus,
    that I may be prepared for every duty,
            love thee in all my mercies,
            submit to thee in every trial,
            trust thee when walking in darkness,
            have peace in thee amidst life's changes.
Lord, I believe, help thou my unbelief and uncertainties.

III
Penitence and Deprecation

SELF-KNOWLEDGE

SEARCHER OF HEARTS,
It is a good day to me when thou givest me
    a glimpse of myself;
Sin is my greatest evil,
    but thou art my greatest good;
I have cause to loathe myself,
    and not to seek self-honour,
    for no one desires to commend his own dunghill.
My country, family, church
    fare worse because of my sins,
    for sinners bring judgment in thinking sins are small,
        or that God is not angry with them.
Let me not take other good men as my example,
    and think I am good because I am like them,
For all good men are not so good as thou desirest,
        are not always consistent,
        do not always follow holiness,
        do not feel eternal good in sore affliction.
Show me how to know when a thing is evil
      which I think is right and good,
      how to know when what is lawful
      comes from an evil principle,
      such as desire for reputation or wealth by usury.
Give me grace to recall my needs,
    my lack of knowing thy will in Scripture,
        of wisdom to guide others,
        of daily repentance, want of which keeps thee at bay,
        of the spirit of prayer, having words without love,
        of zeal for thy glory, seeking my own ends,
        of joy in thee and thy will,
        of love to others.
And let me not lay my pipe too short of the fountain,
            never touching the eternal spring,
            never drawing down water from above.

YET I SIN

ETERNAL FATHER,
Thou art good beyond all thought,
But I am vile, wretched, miserable, blind;
My lips are ready to confess, but my heart is slow to feel,
    and my ways reluctant to amend.
I bring my soul to thee;
    break it, wound it, bend it, mould it.
Unmask to me sin's deformity,
    that I may hate it, abhor it, flee from it.
My faculties have been a weapon of revolt against thee;
    as a rebel I have misused my strength,
    and served the foul adversary of thy kingdom.
Give me grace to bewail my insensate folly,
Grant me to know that the way of transgressors is hard,
        that evil paths are wretched paths,
        that to depart from thee is to lose all good.
I have seen the purity and beauty of thy perfect law,
    the happiness of those in whose heart it reigns,
    the calm dignity of the walk to which it calls,
        yet I daily violate and contemn its precepts.
Thy loving Spirit strives within me,
        brings me Scripture warnings,
        speaks in startling providences,
        allures by secret whispers,
          yet I choose devices and desires to my own hurt,
           impiously resent, grieve,
             and provoke him to abandon me.

All these sins I mourn, lament, and for them cry pardon.
Work in me more profound and abiding repentance;
Give me the fullness of a godly grief that trembles and fears,
    yet ever trusts and loves,
    which is ever powerful, and ever confident;
Grant that through the tears of repentance I may see more clearly
    the brightness and glories of the saving cross.

THE DARK GUEST

O LORD,
Bend my hands and cut them off,
 for I have often struck thee with a wayward will,
 when these fingers should embrace thee by faith.
I am not yet weaned from all created glory,
 honour, wisdom, and esteem of others,
 for I have a secret motive to eye my name in all I do.
Let me not only speak the word sin, but see the thing itself.
Give me to view a discovered sinfulness,
  to know that though my sins are crucified
   they are never wholly mortified.
Hatred, malice, ill-will,
 vain-glory that hungers for and hunts after
  man's approval and applause,
 all are crucified, forgiven,
  but they rise again in my sinful heart.
O my crucified but never wholly mortified sinfulness!
O my life-long damage and daily shame!
O my indwelling and besetting sins!
O the tormenting slavery of a sinful heart!
Destroy, O God, the dark guest within
 whose hidden presence makes my life a hell.
Yet thou hast not left me here without grace;
The cross still stands and meets my needs
 in the deepest straits of the soul. ·
I thank thee that my remembrance of it
 is like David's sight of Goliath's sword
  which preached forth thy deliverance.
The memory of my great sins, my many temptations, my falls,
 bring afresh into my mind the remembrance
  of thy great help, of thy support from heaven,
  of the great grace that saved such a wretch as I am.
There is no treasure so wonderful
 as that continuous experience of thy grace toward me
 which alone can subdue the risings of sin within:
Give me more of it.

[71]

PARADOXES

O CHANGELESS GOD,
Under the conviction of thy Spirit I learn that
>> the more I do, the worse I am,
>> the more I know, the less I know,
>> the more holiness I have, the more sinful I am,
>> the more I love, the more there is to love.
>>> O wretched man that I am!
O Lord,
> I have a wild heart,
>> and cannot stand before thee;
I am like a bird before a man.
How little I love thy truth and ways!
I neglect prayer,
>> by thinking I have prayed enough and earnestly,
>> by knowing thou hast saved my soul.
Of all hypocrites, grant that I may not be an evangelical hypocrite,
>> who sins more safely because grace abounds,
>> who tells his lusts that Christ's blood cleanseth them,
>> who reasons that God cannot cast him into hell, for he is saved,
>> who loves evangelical preaching, churches, Christians, but lives
>>> unholily.
My mind is a bucket without a bottom,
>> with no spiritual understanding,
>> no desire for the Lord's Day,
>> ever learning but never reaching the truth,
>> always at the gospel-well but never holding water.
My conscience is without conviction or contrition,
>> with nothing to repent of.
My will is without power of decision or resolution.
>> My heart is without affection, and full of leaks.
My memory has no retention,
>> so I forget easily the lessons learned,
>> and thy truths seep away.
Give me a broken heart that yet carries home the water of grace.

HEART CORRUPTIONS

O GOD,
May thy Spirit speak in me that I may speak to thee.
I have no merit, let the merit of Jesus stand for me.
I am undeserving, but I look to thy tender mercy.
I am full of infirmities, wants, sin; thou art full of grace.
I confess my sin, my frequent sin, my wilful sin;
All my powers of body and soul are defiled:
A fountain of pollution is deep within my nature.
There are chambers of foul images within my being;
I have gone from one odious room to another,
      walked in a no-man's-land of dangerous imaginations,
        pried into the secrets of my fallen nature.
I am utterly ashamed that I am what I am in myself;
I have no green shoot in me nor fruit, but thorns and thistles;
I am a fading leaf that the wind drives away;
I live bare and barren as a winter tree,
      unprofitable, fit to be hewn down and burnt.
Lord, dost thou have mercy on me?
Thou hast struck a heavy blow at my pride,
    at the false god of self,
      and I lie in pieces before thee.
But thou hast given me another master and lord, thy Son, Jesus,
    and now my heart is turned towards holiness,
        my life speeds as an arrow from a bow
          towards complete obedience to thee.
Help me in all my doings to put down sin and to humble pride.
Save me from the love of the world and the pride of life,
      from everything that is natural to fallen man,
        and let Christ's nature be seen in me day by day.
Grant me grace to bear thy will without repining, and delight to be
    not only chiselled, squared, or fashioned,
      but separated from the old rock where I have been embedded so
        long,
    and lifted from the quarry to the upper air,
      where I may be built in Christ for ever.

SELF-DEPRECATION

O LORD,
My every sense, member, faculty, affection,
    is a snare to me,
I can scarce open my eyes but I envy those above me,
    or despise those below.
I covet honour and riches of the mighty,
    and am proud and unmerciful to the rags of others;
If I behold beauty it is a bait to lust,
    or see deformity, it stirs up loathing and disdain;
How soon do slanders, vain jests, and wanton speeches
    creep into my heart!
Am I comely? what fuel for pride!
Am I deformed? what an occasion for repining!
Am I gifted? how I lust after applause!
Am I unlearned! how I despise what I have not!
Am I in authority? how prone to abuse my trust,
    make will my law, exclude others' enjoyments,
    serve my own interests and policy!
Am I inferior? how much I grudge others' pre-eminence!
Am I rich? how exalted I become!
Thou knowest that all these are snares by my corruptions,
    and that my greatest snare is myself.
I bewail that my apprehensions are dull,
        my thoughts mean,
        my affections stupid,
        my expressions low,
        my life unbeseeming;
Yet what canst thou expect of dust but levity,
                of corruption but defilement?
Keep me ever mindful of my natural state,
    but let me not forget my heavenly title,
    or the grace that can deal with every sin.

THE DEEPS

LORD JESUS,
Give me a deeper repentance,
  a horror of sin,
  a dread of its approach;
Help me chastely to flee it,
  and jealously to resolve that my heart shall be thine alone.
Give me a deeper trust,
  that I may lose myself to find myself in thee,
   the ground of my rest,
   the spring of my being.
Give me a deeper knowledge of thyself
  as saviour, master, lord, and king.
Give me deeper power in private prayer,
   more sweetness in thy Word,
   more steadfast grip on its truth.
Give me deeper holiness in speech, thought, action,
  and let me not seek moral virtue apart from thee.
Plough deep in me, great Lord, heavenly husbandman,
  that my being may be a tilled field,
  the roots of grace spreading far and wide,
   until thou alone art seen in me,
   thy beauty golden like summer harvest,
   thy fruitfulness as autumn plenty.
I have no master but thee,
  no law but thy will,
  no delight but thyself,
  no wealth but that thou givest,
  no good but that thou blessest,
  no peace but that thou bestowest.
I am nothing but that thou makest me,
I have nothing but that I receive from thee,
I can be nothing but that grace adorns me.
Quarry me deep, dear Lord,
  and then fill me to overflowing with living water.

CONTINUAL REPENTANCE

O GOD OF GRACE,
Thou hast imputed my sin to my substitute,
    and hast imputed his righteousness to my soul,
        clothing me with a bridegroom's robe,
        decking me with jewels of holiness.
But in my Christian walk I am still in rags;
    my best prayers are stained with sin;
    my penitential tears are so much impurity;
    my confessions of wrong are so many aggravations of sin;
    my receiving the Spirit is tinctured with selfishness.

I need to repent of my repentance;
I need my tears to be washed;
I have no robe to bring to cover my sins,
    no loom to weave my own righteousness;
I am always standing clothed in filthy garments,
    and by grace am always receiving change of raiment,
    for thou dost always justify the ungodly;
I am always going into the far country,
    and always returning home as a prodigal,
    always saying, Father, forgive me,
    and thou art always bringing forth the best robe.
Every morning let me wear it,
    every evening return in it,
    go out to the day's work in it,
    be married in it,
    be wound in death in it,
    stand before the great white throne in it,
    enter heaven in it shining as the sun.
Grant me never to lose sight of
    the exceeding sinfulness of sin,
    the exceeding righteousness of salvation,
    the exceeding glory of Christ,
    the exceeding beauty of holiness,
    the exceeding wonder of grace.

CONFESSION AND PETITION

HOLY LORD,
I have sinned times without number,
  and been guilty of pride and unbelief,
            of failure to find thy mind in thy Word,
            of neglect to seek thee in my daily life.
My transgressions and short-comings
    present me with a list of accusations,
But I bless thee that they will not stand against me,
    for all have been laid on Christ;
Go on to subdue my corruptions,
    and grant me grace to live above them.
Let not the passions of the flesh nor lustings of the mind
     bring my spirit into subjection,
     but do thou rule over me in liberty and power.
I thank thee that many of my prayers have been refused—
    I have asked amiss and do not have,
    I have prayed from lusts and been rejected,
    I have longed for Egypt and been given a wilderness.
Go on with thy patient work,
    answering 'no' to my wrongful prayers, and fitting me to
      accept it.
Purge me from every false desire, every base aspiration,
    everything contrary to thy rule.
I thank thee for thy wisdom and thy love,
    for all the acts of discipline to which I am subject,
    for sometimes putting me into the furnace
     to refine my gold and remove my dross.

No trial is so hard to bear as a sense of sin.
If thou shouldst give me choice to live in pleasure and keep my sins,
    or to have them burnt away with trial,
    give me sanctified affliction.
Deliver me from every evil habit, every accretion of former sins,
    everything that dims the brightness of thy grace in me,
    everything that prevents me taking delight in thee.
Then I shall bless thee, God of Jeshurun, for helping me to be upright.

CONTRITION

O THOU MOST HIGH,
It becomes me to be low in thy presence.
I am nothing compared with thee;
I possess not the rank and power of angels,
        but thou hast made me what I am,
        and placed me where I am;
    help me to acquiesce in thy sovereign pleasure.
I thank thee that in the embryo state of my endless being
        I am capable by grace of improvement;
        that I can bear thy image,
        not by submissiveness, but by design,
    and can work with thee and advance thy cause and glory.
But, alas, the crown has fallen from my head:
        I have sinned;
        I am alien to thee;
        my head is deceitful and wicked,
        my mind an enemy to thy law.
Yet, in my lostness thou hast laid help on the mighty one
        and he comes between to put his hands on us both,
        my umpire, daysman, mediator,
        whose blood is my peace,
        whose righteousness is my strength,
        whose condemnation is my freedom,
        whose Spirit is my power,
        whose heaven is my heritage.
Grant that I may feel more the strength of thy grace
        in subduing the evil of my nature,
        in loosing me from the present evil world,
        in supporting me under the trials of life,
        in enabling me to abide with thee in my valleys,
        in exercising me to have a conscience void of offence
            before thee and before men.
In all my affairs may I distinguish between duty and anxiety,
and may my character and not my circumstances chiefly engage me.

HUMILIATION

SOVEREIGN LORD,
When clouds of darkness, atheism, and unbelief come to me,
   I see thy purpose of love
        in withdrawing the Spirit that I might prize him more.
        in chastening me for my confidence in past successes,
      that my wound of secret godlessness might be cured.
Help me to humble myself before thee
        by seeing the vanity of honour as a conceit of men's minds,
          as standing between me and thee;
        by seeing that thy will must alone be done,
          as much in denying as in giving spiritual enjoyments;
        by seeing that my heart is nothing but evil,
          mind, mouth, life void of thee;
        by seeing that sin and Satan are allowed power in me
          that I might know my sin, be humbled,
          and gain strength thereby;
        by seeing that unbelief shuts thee from me,
          so that I sense not thy majesty, power, mercy, or love.
Then possess me, for thou only art good and worthy.

Thou dost not play in convincing me of sin,
Satan did not play in tempting me to it,
I do not play when I sink in deep mire,
      for sin is no game, no toy, no bauble;
Let me never forget that the heinousness of sin
      lies not so much in the nature of the sin committed,
         as in the greatness of the person sinned against.
When I am afraid of evils to come, comfort me, by showing me
      that in myself I am a dying, condemned wretch,
        but that in Christ I am reconciled, made alive, and satisfied;
      that I am feeble and unable to do any good,
        but that in him I can do all things;
      that what I now have in Christ is mine in part,
        but that shortly I shall have it perfectly in heaven.

MORTIFICATION

O DIVINE LAWGIVER,
I take shame to myself
      for open violations of thy law,
      for my secret faults,
         my omissions of duty,
         my unprofitable attendance upon means of grace,
         my carnality in worshipping thee,
         and all the sins of my holy things.
My iniquities are increased over my head:
My trespasses are known in the heavens,
    and there Christ is gone also,
         my advocate with the Father,
         my propitiation for sins,
         and I hear his word of peace.
At present it is a day of small things with me,
    I have light enough to see my darkness,
        sensibility enough to feel the hardness of my heart,
        spirituality enough to mourn my want of a heavenly mind;
    but I might have had more,
      I ought to have had more,
      I have never been straitened in thee,
      thou hast always placed before me an infinite fullness,
      and I have not taken it.
I confess and bewail my deficiencies and backslidings:
I mourn my numberless failures,
      my incorrigibility under rebukes,
      my want of profiting under ordinances of mercy,
      my neglect of opportunities for usefulness.
It is not with me as in months past;
O recall me to thyself, and enable me to feel my first love.
May my improvements correspond with my privileges,
May my will accept the decisions of my judgment,
    my choice be that which conscience approves,
and may I never condemn myself in the things I allow!

PURIFICATION

LORD JESUS,
I sin—
Grant that I may never cease grieving because of it,
               never be content with myself,
               never think I can reach a point of perfection.
Kill my envy, command my tongue, trample down self.
Give me grace to be holy, kind, gentle, pure, peaceable,
          to live for thee and not for self,
          to copy thy words, acts, spirit,
          to be transformed into thy likeness,
          to be consecrated wholly to thee,
          to live entirely to thy glory.
Deliver me from attachment to things unclean,
          from wrong associations,
          from the predominance of evil passions,
          from the sugar of sin as well as its gall,
       that with self-loathing, deep contrition,
             earnest heart searching
             I may come to thee, cast myself on thee,
             trust in thee, cry to thee,
             be delivered by thee.
   O God, the Eternal All, help me to know
          that all things are shadows, but thou art substance,
             all things are quicksands, but thou art mountain,
             all things are shifting, but thou art anchor,
             all things are ignorance, but thou art wisdom.
If my life is to be a crucible amid burning heat, so be it,
          but do thou sit at the furnace mouth
          to watch the ore that nothing be lost.
If I sin wilfully, grievously, tormentedly, in grace
          take away my mourning and give me music;
          remove my sackcloth and clothe me with beauty;
          still my sighs and fill my mouth with song,
          then give me summer weather as a Christian.

REPROOFS

O MERCIFUL GOD,
When I hear of disagreeable things amongst Christians,
    it brings an additional weight and burden on my spirit;
I come to thee in my distress and make lamentable complaint;
Teach me how to take reproofs from friends,
    even though I think I do not deserve them;
Use them to make me tenderly afraid of sin,
    more jealous over myself,
    more concerned to keep heart and life unblameable;
Cause them to help me reflect on my want of spirituality,
    to abhor myself,
    to look upon myself as unworthy,
    and make them beneficial to my soul.
May all thy people know how little, mean, and vile I am,
    that they may see I am nothing,
    less than nothing,
    to be accounted nothing,
    that so they may pray for me aright,
    and have not the least dependence upon me.
It is sweet to be nothing and have nothing,
    and to be fed with crumbs from thy hands.
Blessed be thy name for anything that life brings.
    How do poor souls live who have not thee,
    or when helpless have no God to go to,
    who feel not the constraining force of thy love,
    and the sweetness of communion?
O how admirably dost thou captivate the soul,
    making all desires and affections centre on thee!
Give me such vivacity in religion,
    that I may be able to take all reproofs from other men
    as from thy hands,
    and glorify thee for them
    from a sense of thy beneficent love
    and of my need to have my pride destroyed.

THE BROKEN HEART

O LORD,
No day of my life has passed
      that has not proved me guilty in thy sight.
Prayers have been uttered from a prayerless heart;
Praise has been often praiseless sound;
My best services are filthy rags.
Blessed Jesus, let me find a covert in thy appeasing wounds.
Though my sins rise to heaven thy merits soar above them;
Though unrighteousness weighs me down to hell,
thy righteousness exalts me to thy throne.
All things in me call for my rejection,
All things in thee plead my acceptance.
I appeal from the throne of perfect justice
      to thy throne of boundless grace,
Grant me to hear thy voice assuring me:
      that by thy stripes I am healed,
      that thou wast bruised for my iniquities,
      that thou hast been made sin for me
        that I might be righteous in thee,
      that my grievous sins, my manifold sins,
        are all forgiven,
        buried in the ocean of thy concealing blood.
I am guilty, but pardoned,
      lost, but saved,
      wandering, but found,
      sinning, but cleansed.
Give me perpetual broken-heartedness,
Keep me always clinging to thy cross,
Flood me every moment with descending grace,
Open to me the springs of divine knowledge,
      sparkling like crystal,
      flowing clear and unsullied
      through my wilderness of life.

SELF-NOUGHTING

O LORD,
Help me to approach thee
    with becoming conception of thy nature, relations and designs.
Thou inhabitest eternity, and
    my life is nothing before thee;
Thou dwellest in the highest heaven and this cannot contain thee;
    I live in a house of clay.
Thy power is almighty;
    I am crushed before the moth.
Thy understanding is infinite;
    I know nothing as I ought to know.
Thou canst not behold evil;
    I am vile.
In my ignorance, weakness, fears, depressions,
    may thy Spirit help my infirmities
      with supplies of wisdom, strength and comfort.
Let me faithfully study my character,
    be willing to bring it to light,
    observe myself in my trials,
    judge the reality and degree of my grace,
    consider how I have been ensnared or overcome.
Grant that I may never trust my heart,
        depend upon any past experiences,
        magnify any present resolutions,
          but be strong in the grace of Jesus;
    that I may know how to obtain relief from a guilty conscience
    without feeling reconciled to my imperfections.
Sustain me under my trials and improve them to me;
    give me grace to rest in thee,
    and assure me of deliverance.
May I always combine thy majesty with thy mercy,
    and connect thy goodness with thy greatness.
Then shall my heart always rejoice in praises to thee.

SHORTCOMINGS

O LIVING GOD,
I bless thee
> that I see the worst of my heart as well as the best of it,
> that I can sorrow for those sins that carry me from thee,
> that it is thy deep and dear mercy to threaten punishment
>> so that I may return, pray, live.

My sin is to look on my faults and be discouraged,
> or to look on my good and be puffed up.

I fall short of thy glory every day by spending hours unprofitably,
> by thinking that the things I do are good,
>> when they are not done to thy end,
>> nor spring from the rules of thy Word.

My sin is to fear what never will be;
I forget to submit to thy will, and fail to be quiet there.
But Scripture teaches me that thy active will
> reveals a steadfast purpose on my behalf,
> and this quietens my soul, and makes me love thee.

Keep me always in the understanding
> that saints mourn more for sin than other men,
> for when they see how great is thy wrath against sin,
> and how Christ's death alone pacifies that wrath,
> that makes them mourn the more.

Help me to see that although I am in the wilderness
> it is not all briars and barrenness.

I have bread from heaven, streams from the rock,
> light by day, fire by night,
> thy dwelling place and thy mercy seat.

I am sometimes discouraged by the way,
> but though winding and trying it is safe and short;

Death dismays me, but my great high priest stands in its waters,
> and will open me a passage,
> and beyond is a better country.

While I live let my life be exemplary,
When I die may my end be peace.

BACKSLIDING

O LORD,
When the world's unbelievers reject thee,
    and are so forsaken by thee that thou callest them no more,
    it is to thine own thou dost turn,
    for in such seasons of general apostasy
        they in some measure backslide with the world.
O how free is thy grace
    that reminds them of the danger that confronts them
    and urges them to persevere in adherence to thyself!
I bless thee that those who turn aside
    may return to thee immediately,
    and be welcomed without anything to commend them,
    notwithstanding all their former backslidings.
I confess that this is suited to my case, for of late
    I have found great want,
        and lack of apprehension of divine grace;
    I have been greatly distressed of soul
        because I did not suitably come to the fountain
        that purges away all sin;
    I have laboured too much for spiritual life,
        peace of conscience, progressive holiness,
        in my own strength.
I beg thee, show me the arm of all might;
Give me to believe
    that thou canst do for me more than I ask or think,
    and that, though I backslide, thy love will never let me go,
    but will draw me back to thee with everlasting cords;
    that thou dost provide grace in the wilderness,
        and canst bring me out, leaning on the arm of my beloved;
    that thou canst cause me to walk with him
        by the rivers of waters in a straight way,
        wherein I shall not stumble.
Keep me solemn, devout, faithful, resting on free grace
    for assistance, acceptance, and peace of conscience.

SINS

MERCIFUL LORD,
Pardon all my sins of this day, week, year,
    all the sins of my life,
      sins of early, middle, and advanced years,
         of omission and commission,
         of morose, peevish and angry tempers,
         of lip, life and walk,
         of hard-heartedness, unbelief, presumption, pride,
         of unfaithfulness to the souls of men,
         of want of bold decision in the cause of Christ,
         of deficiency in outspoken zeal for his glory,
         of bringing dishonour upon thy great name,
         of deception, injustice, untruthfulness
           in my dealings with others,
         of impurity in thought, word and deed,
         of covetousness, which is idolatry,
         of substance unduly hoarded, improvidently squandered,
           not consecrated to the glory of thee, the great giver;
      sins in private and in the family,
         in study and recreation, in the busy haunts of men,
         in the study of thy Word and in the neglect of it,
         in prayer irreverently offered and coldly withheld,
         in time misspent,
         in yielding to Satan's wiles,
         in opening my heart to his temptations,
         in being unwatchful when I know him nigh,
         in quenching the Holy Spirit;
      sins against light and knowledge,
         against conscience and the restraints of thy Spirit,
         against the law of eternal love.
Pardon all my sins, known and unknown, felt and unfelt,
              confessed and not confessed,
              remembered or forgotten.
Good Lord, hear; and hearing, forgive.

PRIDE

O THOU TERRIBLE MEEK,
Let not pride swell my heart.
My nature is the mire beneath my feet,
        the dust to which I shall return.
In body I surpass not the meanest reptile;
Whatever difference of form and intellect is mine,
        is a free grant of thy goodness;
Every faculty of mind and body is thy undeserved gift.
Low as I am as a creature, I am lower as a sinner;
I have trampled thy law times without number;
Sin's deformity is stamped upon me,
        darkens my brow, touches me with corruption:
How can I flaunt myself proudly?
Lowest abasement is my due place,
        for I am less than nothing before thee.
Help me to see myself in thy sight,
    then pride must wither, decay, die, perish.
Humble my heart before thee,
    and replenish it with thy choicest gifts.
As water rests not on barren hill summits,
        but flows down to fertilize lowest vales,
So make me the lowest of the lowly,
        that my spiritual riches may exceedingly abound.
When I leave duties undone,
        may condemning thought strip me of pride,
        deepen in me devotion to thy service,
        and quicken me to more watchful care.
When I am tempted to think highly of myself,
        grant me to see the wily power of my spiritual enemy;
Help me to stand with wary eye on the watch-tower of faith,
        and to cling with determined grasp to my humble Lord;
If I fall let me hide myself in my redeemer's righteousness,
    and when I escape, may I ascribe all deliverance to thy grace.
Keep me humble, meek, lowly.

PASSION

HOLY LORD,
How little repentance there is in the world,
    and how many sins I have to repent of!
I am troubled for my sin of passion,
    for the shame and horror of it as an evil;
I purpose to give way to it no more,
    and come to thee for strength to that end.
Most men give vent to anger frequently and are overcome by it,
    bringing many excuses and attentuation for it,
      as that it occurs suddenly,
        that they delight not in it,
        that they are sorry afterwards,
        that godly men commit it.
They thus seek peace after outbursts of passion
    by entire forgetfulness of it,
    or, by skimming over their wound, they hope for healing
      without peace in Christ's blood.
Lord God, I know that my sudden anger arises
    when things cross me,
    and I desire to please only myself, not Christ;
There is in all wrongs and crosses a double cross—
    that which crosses me,
    and that which crosses thee;
In all good things there is somewhat that pleases me,
      somewhat that pleases thee;
My sin is that my heart is pleased or troubled
    as things please or trouble me,
    without my having a regard to Christ;
Thus, I am like Eli,
    the subject of punishment for not rebuking sin;
    whereas I should humbly confess my sin
    and fly to the blood of Christ for pardon and peace.
Give me, then, repentance, true brokenness, lasting contrition,
    for these things thou wilt not despise in spite of my sin.

PENITENCE

O LORD OF GRACE,
I have been hasty and short in private prayer,
O quicken my conscience to feel this folly,
                    to bewail this ingratitude;
My first sin of the day leads into others,
    and it is just that thou shouldst withdraw thy presence
    from one who waited carelessly on thee.
Keep me at all times from robbing thee,
    and from depriving my soul of thy due worship;
Let me never forget
    that I have an eternal duty to love, honour and obey thee,
    that thou art infinitely worthy of such;
    that if I fail to glorify thee
        I am guilty of infinite evil that merits infinite punishment,
    for sin is the violation of an infinite obligation.
O forgive me if I have dishonoured thee,
Melt my heart, heal my backslidings,
    and open an intercourse of love.
When the fire of thy compassion warms my inward man,
    and the outpourings of thy Spirit fill my soul,
        then I feelingly wonder at my own depravity,
            and deeply abhor myself;
        then thy grace is a powerful incentive to repentance,
            and an irresistible motive to inward holiness.
May I never forget
That thou hast my heart in thy hands.
Apply to it the merits of Christ's atoning blood whenever I sin.
Let thy mercies draw me to thyself.
Wean me from all evil, mortify me to the world,
    and make me ready for my departure hence
    animated by the humiliations of pentential love.
My soul is often a chariot without wheels,
    clogged and hindered in sin's miry clay;
Mount it on eagle's wings and cause it to soar upward to thyself.

MAN A NOTHING

O LORD,
I am a shell full of dust,
    but animated with an invisible rational soul
    and made anew by an unseen power of grace;
Yet I am no rare object of valuable price,
    but one that has nothing and is nothing,
    although chosen of thee from eternity,
        given to Christ,and born again;
I am deeply convinced of the evil and misery of a sinful state,
    of the vanity of creatures,
    but also of the sufficiency of Christ.
When thou wouldst guide me I control myself,
When thou wouldst be sovereign I rule myself.
When thou wouldst take care of me I suffice myself.
When I should depend on thy providings I supply myself,
When I should submit to thy providence I follow my will,
When I should study, love, honour, trust thee, I serve myself;
I fault and correct thy laws to suit myself,
Instead of thee I look to man's approbation,
    and am by nature an idolater.
Lord, it is my chief design to bring my heart back to thee.
Convince me that I cannot be my own god, or make myself happy,
    nor my own Christ to restore my joy,
    nor my own Spirit to teach, guide, rule me.
Help me to see that grace does this by providential affliction,
    for when my credit is god thou·dost cast me lower,
    when riches are my idol thou dost wing them away,
    when pleasure is my all thou dost turn it into bitterness.
Take away my roving eye, curious ear, greedy appetite, lustful heart;
Show me that none of these things
    can heal a wounded conscience,
    or support a tottering frame,
    or uphold a departing spirit.
Then take me to the cross and leave me there.

A CRY FOR DELIVERANCE

HEAVENLY FATHER,
Save me entirely from sin.
I know I am righteous through the righteousness of another,
      but I pant and pine for likeness to thyself;
I am thy child and should bear thy image,
Enable me to recognize my death unto sin;
When it tempts me may I be deaf unto its voice.
Deliver me from the invasion as well as the dominion of sin.
Grant me to walk as Christ walked,
        to live in the newness of his life,
            the life of love, the life of faith,
            the life of holiness.
I abhor my body of death,
      its indolence, envy, meanness, pride.
Forgive, and kill these vices,
      have mercy on my unbelief,
          on my corrupt and wandering heart.
When thy blessings come I begin to idolize them,
      and set my affection on some beloved object—
      children, friends, wealth, honour;
Cleanse this spiritual adultery and give me chastity;
      close my heart to all but thee.
Sin is my greatest curse;
Let thy victory be apparent to my consciousness,
      and displayed in my life.
Help me to be always devoted, confident, obedient,
        resigned, childlike in my trust of thee,
      to love thee with soul, body, mind, strength,
      to love my fellow-man as I love myself,
      to be saved from unregenerate temper, hard thoughts,
        slanderous words, meanness, unkind manners,
      to master my tongue and keep the door of my lips.
Fill me with grace daily,
      that my life be a fountain of sweet water.

MERCY

GOD OF THE PUBLICAN,
Be merciful to me a sinner;
  this I am by nature and practice,
  this thy word proclaims me to be,
  this I hope I feel myself to be;
Yet thou hast not left me to despair,
  for there is no 'peradventure' in thy grace;
I have all the assurance I need
  that with thee is plenteous redemption.

In spite of the number and heinousness of my sins
  thou hast given me a token for good;
The golden sceptre is held out,
  and thou hast said 'Touch it and live'.
May I encourage myself by a sense of thy all-sufficiency,
     by faith in thy promises,
     by views of the experience of others.
To that dear refuge in which so many have sheltered from every storm
    may I repair,
In that fountain always freely open for sin
     may I be cleansed from every defilement.
Sin is that abominable thing which thy soul hates,
  and this alone separates thee and me.
Thou canst not contradict the essential perfections of thy nature;
Thou canst not make me happy *with* thyself,
  till thou hast made me holy *like* thyself.

O holy God, make me such a creature as thou canst take pleasure in,
  and such a being that I can take pleasure in thee.
May I consent to and delight in thy law after the inner man,
  never complain over the strictness of thy demands,
    but mourn over my want of conformity to them;
  never to question thy commandments,
    but esteem them to be right.
By thy Spirit within me may my practice spring from principle, and
      my dispositions be conformable with
    duty.

CRUCIFIXION AND RESURRECTION

O LORD,
I marvel that thou shouldst become incarnate,
    be crucified, dead, and buried.
The sepulchre calls forth my adoring wonder,
    for it is empty and thou art risen;
    the four-fold gospel attests it,
    the living witnesses prove it,
    my heart's experience knows it.
Give me to die with thee that I may rise to new life,
    for I wish to be as dead and buried
        to sin, to selfishness, to the world;
    that I might not hear the voice of the charmer,
        and might be delivered from his lusts.
O Lord, there is much ill about me – crucify it,
        much flesh within me – mortify it.
Purge me from selfishness, the fear of man, the love of approbation,
        the shame of being thought old-fashioned,
        the desire to be cultivated or modern.
Let me reckon my old life dead because of crucifixion,
    and never feed it as a living thing.
Grant me to stand with my dying Saviour,
      to be content to be rejected,
      to be willing to take up unpopular truths,
        and to hold fast despised teachings until death.
Help me to be resolute and Christ-contained.
Never let me wander from the path of obedience to thy will.
Strengthen me for the battles ahead.
Give me courage for all the trials, and grace for all the joys.
Help me to be a holy, happy person,
    free from every wrong desire,
        from everything contrary to thy mind.
Grant me more and more of the resurrection life:
    may it rule me,
    may I walk in its power, and be strengthened through its influence.

NEW BEGINNING

INCOMPREHENSIBLE, GREAT, AND GLORIOUS GOD,
I adore thee and abase myself.
I approach thee mindful that I am less than nothing,
  a creature worse than nothing.
My thoughts are not screened from thy gaze,
My secret sins blaze in the light of thy countenance.
Enable me to remember that blood which cleanseth all sin,
   to believe in that grace which subdues all iniquities,
   to resign myself to that agency
    which can deliver me from the bondage of corruption
    into the glorious liberty of the sons of God.
Thou hast begun a good work in me
  and canst alone continue and complete it.
Give me an increasing conviction of my tendency to err,
  and of my exposure to sin.
Help me to feel more of the purifying, softening influence of religion,
  its compassion, love, pity, courtesy,
  and employ me as thy instrument
   in blessing others.
Give me to distinguish between the mere form of godliness and its
     power,
    between life and a name to live,
    between guile and truth,
    between hypocrisy and a religion
     that will bear thy eye.
If I am not right, set me right, keep me right;
And may I at last come to thy house in peace.

RELIANCE

MY FATHER,
When thou art angry towards me for my wrongs
     I try to pacify thee by abstaining from future sin;
But teach me that I cannot satisfy thy law,
         that this effort is a resting in my righteousness,
         that only Christ's righteousness,
            ready made, already finished,
            is fit for that purpose;
            that thy chastising me for my sin
            is not that I should try to reform,
            but only that I may be more humbled,
            afflicted, and separated from sin,
            by being reconciled,
            and made righteous in Christ by faith;
         that a sense of my sufficiency and ability in him
            is one means of my being immovable;
         that I can never be so by resting on my own faith,
            but by trusting in thee
            as my only support, by faith;
         that if I cast away my faith I cast away thee,
            for by faith I apprehend thee,
            and as thou art very precious,
            so is my faith very precious to me;
         that I fall short of the purity thou requirest,
            because in thinking I am holy
            I do not seek holiness,
            or, believing I am impotent, I do no more.
Humble me for not being as holy as I should be,
     or as holy as I might be through Christ,
     for thou art all, and to possess thee is to possess all.
But to make the creature something
     is to make it stand between thee and me,
     so that I do not walk humbly and holily.
Lord, forgive me for this.

IV
Needs and Devotions

NEED OF GRACE

O LORD,
Thou knowest my great unfitness for service,
        my present deadness,
        my inability to do anything for thy glory,
        my distressing coldness of heart.
I am weak, ignorant, unprofitable,
    and loathe and abhor myself.
I am at a loss to know what thou wouldest have me do,
    for I feel amazingly deserted by thee,
    and sense thy presence so little;
Thou makest me possess the sins of my youth,
    and the dreadful sin of my nature,
    so that I feel all sin,
    I cannot think or act but every motion is sin.
Return again with showers of converting grace
    to a poor gospel-abusing sinner.
Help my soul to breathe after holiness,
    after a constant devotedness to thee,
    after growth in grace more abundantly every day.
O Lord, I am lost in the pursuit of this blessedness,
And am ready to sink because I fall short of my desire;
Help me to hold out a little longer,
    until the happy hour of deliverance comes,
    for I cannot lift my soul to thee
    if thou of thy goodness bring me not nigh.
Help me to be diffident, watchful, tender,
    lest I offend my blessed friend
    in thought and behaviour;
I confide in thee and lean upon thee,
    and need thee at all times to assist and lead me.
O that all my distresses and apprehensions
    might prove but Christ's school
    to make me fit for greater service
    by teaching me the great lesson of humility.

CONFLICT

O LORD GOD,
Thou art my protecting arm,
    fortress, refuge, shield, buckler.
Fight for me and my foes must flee;
Uphold me and I cannot fall;
Strengthen me and I stand unmoved, unmoveable;
Equip me and I shall receive no wound;
Stand by me and Satan will depart;
Anoint my lips with a song of salvation
    and I shall shout thy victory;
Give me abhorrence of all evil,
    as a vile monster that
        defies thy law, casts off thy yoke,
        defiles my nature, spreads misery.
Teach me to look to Jesus on his cross
    and so to know sin's loathsomeness in thy sight.
There is no pardon but through thy Son's death,
    no cleansing but in his precious blood,
    no atonement but his to expiate evil.
Show me the shame, the agony, the bruises of incarnate God,
    that I may read boundless guilt in the boundless price;
May I discern the deadly viper in its real malignity,
    tear it with holy indignation from my breast,
    resolutely turn from its every snare,
    refuse to hold polluting dalliance with it.
Blessed Lord Jesus, at thy cross
    may I be taught the awful miseries from which I am saved,
        ponder what the word 'lost' implies,
        see the fires of eternal destruction;
Then may I cling more closely to thy broken self,
    adhere to thee with firmer faith,
    be devoted to thee with total being,
    detest sin as strongly as thy love to me is strong,
And may holiness be the atmosphere in which I live.

PERIL

SOVEREIGN COMMANDER OF THE UNIVERSE,
I am sadly harassed by doubts, fears, unbelief,
     in a felt spiritual darkness.
My heart is full of evil surmisings and disquietude,
     and I cannot act faith at all.
My heavenly pilot has disappeared,
     and I have lost my hold on the rock of ages;
I sink in deep mire beneath storms and waves,
     in horror and distress unutterable.
Help me, O Lord,
     to throw myself absolutely and wholly on thee,
     for better, for worse, without comfort, and all but hopeless.
Give me peace of soul, confidence, enlargement of mind,
     morning joy that comes after night heaviness;
Water my soul richly with divine blessings;
Grant that I may welcome thy humbling in private
     so that I might enjoy thee in public;
Give me a mountain top as high as the valley is low.
Thy grace can melt the worst sinner, and I am as vile as he;
Yet thou hast made me a monument of mercy,
     a trophy of redeeming power;
In my distress let me not forget this.
All-wise God,
Thy never-failing providence orders every event.
     sweetens every fear,
     reveals evil's presence lurking in seeming good,
     brings real good out of seeming evil,
     makes unsatisfactory what I set my heart upon,
     to show me what a short-sighted creature I am,
     and to teach me to live by faith upon thy blessed self.
Out of my sorrow and night
     give me the name Naphtali – 'satisfied with favour' –
     help me to love thee as thy child,
     and to walk worthy of my heavenly pedigree.

NEED OF JESUS

LORD JESUS,
I am blind, be thou my light,
    ignorant, be thou my wisdom,
    self-willed, be thou my mind.
Open my ear to grasp quickly thy Spirit's voice,
    and delightfully run after his beckoning hand;
Melt my conscience that no hardness remain,
    make it alive to evil's slightest touch;
When Satan approaches may I flee to thy wounds,
    and there cease to tremble at all alarms.
Be my good shepherd to lead me into the green pastures of thy Word,
    and cause me to lie down beside the rivers of its comforts.
Fill me with peace, that no disquieting worldly gales
    may ruffle the calm surface of my soul.
Thy cross was upraised to be my refuge,
Thy blood streamed forth to wash me clean,
Thy death occurred to give me a surety,
Thy name is my property to save me,
By thee all heaven is poured into my heart,
    but it is too narrow to comprehend thy love.
I was a stranger, an outcast, a slave, a rebel,
    but thy cross has brought me near,
            has softened my heart,
            has made me thy Father's child,
            has admitted me to thy family,
            has made me joint-heir with thyself.
O that I may love thee as thou lovest me,
   that I may walk worthy of thee, my Lord,
   that I may reflect the image of heaven's first-born.
May I always see thy beauty with the clear eye of faith,
    and feel the power of thy Spirit in my heart,
    for unless he move mightily in me
    no inward fire will be kindled.

WEAKNESSES

O SPIRIT OF GOD,
Help my infirmities;
When I am pressed down with a load of sorrow,
  perplexed and knowing not what to do,
  slandered and persecuted,
  made to feel the weight of the cross,
   help me, I pray thee.
If thou seest in me any wrong thing encouraged,
   any evil desire cherished,
   any delight that is not thy delight,
   any habit that grieves thee,
   any nest of sin in my heart,
    then grant me the kiss of thy forgiveness,
  and teach my feet to walk the way of thy commandments.
Deliver me from carking care,
  and make me a happy, holy person;
Help me to walk the separated life with firm and brave step,
  and to wrestle successfully against weakness;
Teach me to laud, adore, and magnify thee,
  with the music of heaven,
And make me a perfume of praiseful gratitude to thee.
I do not crouch at thy feet as a slave before a tyrant,
  but exult before thee as a son with a father.
Give me power to live as thy child in all my actions,
  and to exercise sonship by conquering self.
Preserve me from the intoxication that comes of prosperity;
Sober me when I am glad with a joy that comes not from thee.
Lead me safely on to the eternal kingdom,
  not asking whether the road be rough or smooth.
I request only to see the face of him I love,
  to be content with bread to eat,
   with raiment to put on,
  if I can be brought to thy house in peace.

THE INFINITE AND THE FINITE

THOU GREAT *I AM*,
Fill my mind with elevation and grandeur at the thought of a Being
      with whom one day is as a thousand years,
          and a thousand years as one day,
A mighty God who, amidst the lapse of worlds,
      and the revolutions of empires,
      feels no variableness,
      but is glorious in immortality.
May I rejoice that, while men die, the Lord lives;
          that, while all creatures are broken reeds,
                     empty cisterns,
                     fading flowers,
                     withering grass,
          he is the rock of ages, the fountain of living waters.
Turn my heart from vanity,
          from dissatisfactions,
          from uncertainties of the present state,
          to an eternal interest in Christ.
Let me remember that life is short and unforeseen,
      and is only an opportunity for usefulness;
Give me a holy avarice to redeem the time,
      to awake at every call to charity and piety,
      so that I may feed the hungry,
          clothe the naked,
          instruct the ignorant,
          reclaim the vicious,
          forgive the offender,
          diffuse the gospel,
          show neighbourly love to all.
Let me live a life of self-distrust,
          dependence on thyself,
          mortification,
          crucifixion,
          prayer.

CHOICES

O GOD
Though I am allowed to approach thee
      I am not unmindful of my sins,
      I do not deny my guilt,
I confess my wickedness, and earnestly plead forgiveness.

May I with Moses choose affliction rather than enjoy the pleasures of
    sin.
Help me to place myself always under thy guiding and guardian care,
      to take firmer hold of the sure covenant that binds me to thee,
      to feel more of the purifying, dignifying,
        softening influence of the religion I profess,
      to have more compassion, love, pity, courtesy,
      to deem it an honour to be employed by thee
        as an instrument in thy hands,
        ready to seize every opportunity of usefulness,
        and willing to offer all my talents to thy service.

Thou hast done for me all things well,
    hast remembered, distinguished, indulged me.
All my desires have not been gratified,
    but thy love denied them to me
    when fulfilment of my wishes would have proved my ruin or
      injury.
My trials have been fewer than my sins,
    and when I have kissed the rod it has fallen from thy hands.
Thou hast often wiped away my tears,
        restored peace to my mourning heart,
        chastened me for my profit.
All thy work for me is perfect, and I praise thee.

DESIRES

O THOU THAT HEAREST PRAYER,
Teach me to pray.
I confess that in religious exercises
>> the language of my lips and the feelings of my heart
>> have not always agreed,
> that I have frequently taken carelessly upon my tongue
>> a name never pronounced above without reverence and
>>> humility,
> that I have often desired things which would have injured me,
> that I have depreciated some of my chief mercies,
> that I have erred both on the side of my hopes and also of my
>> fears,
> that I am unfit to choose for myself,
>> for it is not in me to direct my steps.
Let thy Spirit help my infirmities,
> for I know not what to pray for as I ought.
Let him produce in me wise desires by which I may ask right things,
> then I shall know thou hearest me.
May I never be importunate for temporal blessings,
> but always refer them to thy fatherly goodness,
> for thou knowest what I need before I ask;
May I never think I prosper unless my soul prospers,
>> or that I am rich unless rich toward thee,
>> or that I am wise unless wise unto salvation.
May I seek first thy kingdom and its righteousness.
May I value things in relation to eternity.
May my spiritual welfare be my chief solicitude.
May I be poor, afflicted, despised and have thy blessing,
> rather than be successful in enterprise,
>> or have more than my heart can wish,
> or be admired by my fellow-men,
>> if thereby these things make me forget thee.
May I regard the world as dreams, lies, vanities, vexation of spirit,
>> and desire to depart from it.
And may I seek my happiness in thy favour, image, presence, service.

FAITH AND THE WORLD

O LORD,
The world is artful to entrap,
      approaches in fascinating guise,
      extends many a gilded bait,
      presents many a charming face.
Let my faith scan every painted bauble,
        and escape every bewitching snare
        in a victory that overcomes all things.
In my duties give me firmness, energy, zeal,
          devotion to thy cause,
          courage in thy name,
          love as a working grace,
        and all commensurate with my trust.
Let faith stride forth in giant power,
        and love respond with energy in every act.
I often mourn the absence of my beloved Lord
      whose smile makes earth a paradise,
      whose voice is sweetest music,
      whose presence gives all graces strength.
But by unbelief I often keep him outside my door.
Let faith give entrance that he may abide with me for ever.

Thy Word is full of promises,
        flowers of sweet fragrance,
        fruit of refreshing flavour
        when culled by faith.
May I be made rich in its riches,
      be strong in its power,
      be happy in its joy.
      abide in its sweetness,
      feast on its preciousness,
      draw vigour from its manna.
Lord, increase my faith.

JOURNEYING ON

LORD OF THE CLOUD AND FIRE,
I am a stranger, with a stranger's indifference;
My hands hold a pilgrim's staff,
My march is Zionward,
My eyes are toward the coming of the Lord,
My heart is in thy hands without reserve.
Thou hast created it,
      redeemed it,
      renewed it,
      captured it,
      conquered it.
Keep from it every opposing foe,
      crush in it every rebel lust,
        mortify every treacherous passion,
        annihilate every earthborn desire.
All faculties of my being vibrate to thy touch;
I love thee with soul, mind, body, strength,
      might, spirit, affection, will,
      desire, intellect, understanding.
Thou art the very perfection of all perfections;
All intellect is derived from thee;
My scanty rivulets flow from thy unfathomable fountain.
Compared with thee the sun is darkness,
         all beauty deformity,
         all wisdom folly,
         the best goodness faulty.
Thou art worthy of an adoration greater than my dull heart can yield;
Invigorate my love that it may rise worthily to thee,
    tightly entwine itself round thee,
    be allured by thee.
Then shall my walk be endless praise.

SPIRITUAL GROWTH

O THOU MOST HIGH,
In the way of thy appointment I am waiting for thee,
  My desire is to thy name,
  My mind to remembrance of thee.
I am a sinner, but not insensible of my state.
My iniquities are great and numberless,
  but thou art adequate to my relief,
    for thou art rich in mercy;
    the blood of thy Son can cleanse from all sin;
    the agency of thy Spirit can subdue my most powerful lusts.
Give me a tender, wakeful conscience
  that can smite and torment me when I sin.
May I be consistent in conversation and conduct,
  the same alone as in company,
      in prosperity and adversity,
      accepting all thy commandments as right,
      and hating every false way.
May I never be satisfied with my present spiritual progress,
  but to faith add virtue, knowledge, temperance, godliness,
        brotherly kindness, charity.
May I never neglect
    what is necessary to constitute Christian character,
    and needful to complete it.
May I cultivate the expedient,
  develop the lovely, adorn the gospel,
  recommend the religion of Jesus,
  accommodate myself to thy providence.

Keep me from sinking or sinning in the evil day;
Help me to carry into ordinary life portions of divine truth
    and use them on suitable occasions, so that
      its doctrines may inform,
      its warnings caution,
      its rules guide,
      its promises comfort me.

VOYAGE

O LORD OF THE OCEANS,
My little bark sails on a restless sea,
Grant that Jesus may sit at the helm and steer me safely;
Suffer no adverse currents to divert my heavenward course;
Let not my faith be wrecked amid storms and shoals;
Bring me to harbour with flying pennants,
            hull unbreached, cargo unspoiled.
I ask great things,
  expect great things,
  shall receive great things.
I venture on thee wholly, fully,
            my wind, sunshine, anchor, defence.
The voyage is long, the waves high, the storms pitiless,
            but my helm is held steady,
            thy Word secures safe passage,
            thy grace wafts me onward,
            my haven is guaranteed.
This day will bring me nearer home,
Grant me holy consistency in every transaction,
            my peace flowing as a running tide,
            my righteousness as every chasing wave.
Help me to live circumspectly,
            with skill to convert every care into prayer,
Halo my path with gentleness and love,
      smooth every asperity of temper;
      let me not forget how easy it is to occasion grief;
      may I strive to bind up every wound,
            and pour oil on all troubled waters.
May the world this day be happier and better because I live.
Let my mast before me be the saviour's cross,
            and every oncoming wave the fountain in his side.
Help me, protect me in the moving sea
            until I reach the shore of unceasing praise.

YEAR'S END

O LOVE BEYOND COMPARE,
Thou art good when thou givest,
          when thou takest away,
          when the sun shines upon me,
          when night gathers over me.
Thou hast loved me before the foundation of the world,
          and in love didst redeem my soul;
Thou dost love me still,
          in spite of my hard heart, ingratitude, distrust.
Thy goodness has been with me during another year,
          leading me through a twisting wilderness,
          in retreat helping me to advance,
          when beaten back making sure headway.
Thy goodness will be with me in the year ahead;
I hoist sail and draw up anchor,
With thee as the blessed pilot of my future as of my past.
I bless thee that thou hast veiled my eyes to the waters ahead.
If thou hast appointed storms of tribulation,
          thou wilt be with me in them;
If I have to pass through tempests of persecution and temptation,
          I shall not drown;
If I am to die,
          I shall see thy face the sooner;
If a painful end is to be my lot,
          grant me grace that my faith fail not;
If I am to be cast aside from the service I love,
          I can make no stipulation;
Only glorify thyself in me whether in comfort or trial,
          as a chosen vessel meet always for thy use.

NEW YEAR

O LORD,
Length of days does not profit me except the days are passed
      in thy presence, in thy service, to thy glory.
Give me a grace that precedes, follows, guides, sustains,
      sanctifies, aids every hour,
   that I may not be one moment apart from thee,
   but may rely on thy Spirit
      to supply every thought,
      speak in every word,
      direct every step,
      prosper every work,
      build up every mote of faith,
      and give me a desire
         to show forth thy praise,
         testify thy love,
         advance thy kingdom.
I launch my bark on the unknown waters of this year,
      with thee, O Father, as my harbour,
         thee, O Son, at my helm,
         thee, O Holy Spirit, filling my sails.
Guide me to heaven with my loins girt,
            my lamp burning,
            my ear open to thy calls,
            my heart full of love,
            my soul free.
Give me thy grace to sanctify me,
      thy comforts to cheer,
      thy wisdom to teach,
      thy right hand to guide,
      thy counsel to instruct,
      thy law to judge,
      thy presence to stabilize.
May thy fear be my awe,
      thy triumphs my joy.

THE FAMILY

O SOVEREIGN LORD,
Thou art the creator-Father of all men, for thou hast made and dost
    support them;
Thou art the special Father of those who know, love and honour thee,
    who find thy yoke easy, and thy burden light,
    thy work honourable,
    thy commandments glorious.
But how little thy undeserved goodness has affected me!
    how imperfectly have I improved my religious privileges!
    how negligent have I been in doing good to others!
I am before thee in my trespasses and sins,
    have mercy on me,
    and may thy goodness bring me to repentance.
Help me to hate and forsake every false way,
    to be attentive to my condition and character,
    to bridle my tongue,
    to keep my heart with all diligence,
    to watch and pray against temptation,
    to mortify sin,
    to be concerned for the salvation of others.
O God, I cannot endure to see the destruction of my kindred.
Let those that are united to me in tender ties
    be precious in thy sight and devoted to thy glory.
Sanctify and prosper my domestic devotion,
    instruction, discipline, example,
    that my house may be a nursery for heaven,
    my church the garden of the Lord,
    enriched with trees of righteousness of thy planting,
    for thy glory;
Let not those of my family who are amiable, moral, attractive,
    fall short of heaven at last;
Grant that the promising appearances of a tender conscience,
    soft heart, the alarms and delights of thy Word,
    be not finally blotted out,
    but bring forth judgment unto victory in all whom I love.

CARING LOVE

ALL-SUFFICIENT KING,
When I come into thy presence I see
    the glory of thy perfections,
    the throne of eternal and universal empire,
    the ten thousand times ten thousand who minister to thee.
Impress my mind with the consciousness of thy greatness,
    not to drive me from thee
        but to inspire me to approach thee;
    not to diminish my confidence in thee,
        but to lead me to admire thy great condescension.
Thou hast been mindful of me and visited me,
        taken charge of me from birth,
        cared in all conditions for me,
        fed me at thy table,
        drawn the curtains of love around me,
        given me new mercies every morning.
Suffer me not to forget that I look for yet greater blessings—
    a hope beyond the grave,
    the earnest and foretastes of immortality,
    holiness, wisdom, strength, peace, joy;
    all these thou hast provided for me in Christ.
I grieve to think how insensible I have been
    of the claims of thy authority,
    and the endearments of thy love;
        how little I have credited thy truth,
            trusted thy promises,
            feared thy threats,
            obeyed thy commands,
            improved my advantages,
            welcomed thy warnings,
            responded to thy grace;
    but notwithstanding my desert I yet live.
May thy goodness always lead me to repentance,
    and thy longsuffering prove my salvation.

DIVINE SUPPORT

THOU ART THE BLESSED GOD,
    happy in thyself,
    source of happiness in thy creatures,
    my maker, benefactor, proprietor, upholder.
Thou hast produced and sustained me,
        supported and indulged me,
        saved and kept me;
Thou art in every situation able to meet my needs and miseries.
May I live by thee,
    live for thee,
      never be satisfied with my Christian progress
        but as I resemble Christ;
And may conformity to his principles, temper, and conduct
    grow hourly in my life.
Let thy unexampled love constrain me into holy obedience,
    and render my duty my delight.
If others deem my faith folly,
        my meekness infirmity,
        my zeal madness,
        my hope delusion,
        my actions hypocrisy,
    may I rejoice to suffer for thy name.
Keep me walking steadfastly towards the country
    of everlasting delights,
    that paradise-land which is my true inheritance.
Support me by the strength of heaven
    that I may never turn back,
    or desire false pleasures
      that wilt and disappear into nothing.
As I pursue my heavenly journey by thy grace
    let me be known as a man with no aim
    but that of a burning desire for thee,
    and the good and salvation of my fellow men.

GRACE ACTIVE

LORD JESUS, GREAT HIGH PRIEST,
Thou hast opened a new and living way
    by which a fallen creature can approach thee with acceptance.
Help me to contemplate the dignity of thy Person,
           the perfectness of thy sacrifice,
           the effectiveness of thy intercession.
O what blessedness accompanies devotion,
    when under all the trials that weary me,
        the cares that corrode me,
        the fears that disturb me,
        the infirmities that oppress me,
    I can come to thee in my need
    and feel peace beyond understanding!
The grace that restores is necessary to preserve,
    lead, guard, supply, help me.
And here thy saints encourage my hope;
    they were once poor and are now rich,
        bound and are now free,
        tried and now are victorious.
Every new duty calls for more grace than I now possess,
    but not more than is found in thee, the divine treasury
    in whom all fullness dwells.
To thee I repair for grace upon grace,
    until every void made by sin be replenished
    and I am filled with all thy fullness.
May my desires be enlarged and my hopes emboldened,
    that I may honour thee by my entire dependency
    and the greatness of my expectation.
Do thou be with me, and prepare me for all
    the smiles of prosperity, the frowns of adversity,
    the losses of substance, the death of friends,
    the days of darkness, the changes of life,
    and the last great change of all.
May I find thy grace sufficient for all my needs.

MORNING

COMPASSIONATE LORD,
Thy mercies have brought me to the dawn of another day,
Vain will be its gift unless I grow in grace,
                    increase in knowledge,
                    ripen for spiritual harvest.
Let me this day know thee as thou art,
           love thee supremely,
           serve thee wholly,
           admire thee fully.
Through grace let my will respond to thee,
Knowing that power to obey is not in me, but
        that thy free love alone enables me to serve thee.
Here then is my empty heart,
        overflow it with thy choicest gifts;
Here is my blind understanding,
        chase away its mists of ignorance.
O ever watchful Shepherd,
        lead, guide, tend me this day;
Without thy restraining rod I err and stray;
Hedge up my path lest I wander into unwholesome pleasure,
        and drink its poisonous streams;
Direct my feet that I be not entangled in Satan's secret snares,
        nor fall into his hidden traps.
Defend me from assailing foes,
          from evil circumstances,
          from myself.
My adversaries are part and parcel of my nature;
They cling to me as my very skin;
I cannot escape their contact.
In my rising up and sitting down they barnacle me;
They entice with constant baits;
My enemy is within the citadel;
Come with almighty power and cast him out, pierce him to death,
  and abolish in me every particle of carnal life this day.

MORNING NEEDS

O GOD, THE AUTHOR OF ALL GOOD,
I come to thee for the grace another day will require
   for its duties and events.
  I step out into a wicked world,
  I carry about with me an evil heart,
  I know that without thee I can do nothing,
    that everything with which I shall be concerned,
     however harmless in itself,
    may prove an occasion of sin or folly,
   unless I am kept by thy power.
Hold thou me up and I shall be safe.
Preserve my understanding from subtilty of error,
  my affections from love of idols,
  my character from stain of vice,
  my profession from every form of evil.
May I engage in nothing in which I cannot implore thy blessing,
  and in which I cannot invite thy inspection.
Prosper me in all lawful undertakings,
  or prepare me for disappointments;
Give me neither poverty nor riches;
Feed me with food convenient for me,
  lest I be full and deny thee
  and say, Who is the Lord?
  or be poor, and steal, and take thy name in vain.
May every creature be made good to me by prayer and thy will;
Teach me how to use the world, and not abuse it,
   to improve my talents,
   to redeem my time,
   to walk in wisdom toward those without,
    and in kindness to those within,
   to do good to all men,
    and especially to my fellow Christians.
And to thee be the glory.

MORNING DEDICATION

ALMIGHTY GOD,
As I cross the threshold of this day
I commit myself, soul, body, affairs, friends, to thy care;
Watch over, keep, guide, direct, sanctify, bless me.
Incline my heart to thy ways;
Mould me wholly into the image of Jesus, as a potter forms clay;
May my lips be a well-tuned harp to sound thy praise;
Let those around see me living by thy Spirit,
                     trampling the world underfoot,
                     unconformed to lying vanities,
                     transformed by a renewed mind,
                     clad in the entire armour of God,
                     shining as a never-dimmed light,
                     showing holiness in all my doings.
Let no evil this day soil my thoughts, words, hands.
May I travel miry paths with a life pure from spot or stain.
In needful transactions let my affection be in heaven,
           and my love soar upwards in flames of fire,
           my gaze fixed on unseen things,
           my eyes open to the emptiness, fragility,
              mockery of earth and its vanities.
May I view all things in the mirror of eternity,
           waiting for the coming of my Lord,
           listening for the last trumpet call,
           hastening unto the new heaven and earth.
Order this day all my communications according to thy wisdom,
           and to the gain of mutual good.
Forbid that I should not be profited or made profitable.
May I speak each word as if my last word,
           and walk each step as my final one.
If my life should end today, let this be my best day.

EVENING PRAYER

O LOVER OF THY PEOPLE,
>   thou hast placed my whole being in the hands of Jesus,
>   my redeemer, commander, husband, friend,
>   and carest for me in him.

Keep me holy, harmless, undefiled, separate from sinners;
May I not know the voice of strangers,
>   but go to him where he is, and follow where he leads.

Thou hast bathed me once for all in the sin-removing fountain,
>   cleanse me now from this day's defilement,
>   from its faults, deficiencies of virtue,
>   harmful extremes,
>   that I may exhibit a perfect character in Jesus.

O master, who didst wash the disciples' feet,
>   be very patient with me,
>   be very condescending to my faults,
>   go on with me till thy great work in me is completed.

I desire to conquer self in every respect,
>   to overcome the body with its affections and lusts,
>   to keep under my flesh,
>   to guard my manhood from all grosser sins,
>   to check the refined power of my natural mind,
>   to live entirely to thy glory,
>   to be deaf to unmerited censure and the praise of men.

Nothing can hurt my new-born inner man,
>   it cannot be smitten or die;

Nothing can mar the dominion of thy Spirit within me;
It is enough to have thy approbation and that of my conscience.
Keep me humble, dependent, supremely joyful,
>   as calm and quiet as a sucking child,
>   yet earnest and active.

I wish not so much to do as to be, and I long to be like Jesus;
If thou dost make me right I shall be right;
Lord, I belong to thee, make me worthy of thyself.

EVENING PRAISE

GIVER OF ALL,
Another day is ended
   and I take my place beneath my great redeemer's cross,
   where healing streams continually descend,
   where balm is poured into every wound,
   where I wash anew in the all-cleansing blood,
   assured that thou seest in me no spots of sin.
Yet a little while and I shall go to thy home and be no more seen;
Help me to gird up the loins of my mind,
   to quicken my step,
   to speed as if each moment were my last,
    that my life be joy, my death glory.
I thank thee for the temporal blessings of this world—
   the refreshing air,
   the light of the sun,
   the food that renews strength,
   the raiment that clothes,
   the dwelling that shelters,
   the sleep that gives rest,
   the starry canopy of night,
   the summer breeze,
   the flowers' sweetness,
   the music of flowing streams,
   the happy endearments of family, kindred, friends.
Things animate, things inanimate, minister to my comfort.
My cup runs over.
Suffer me not to be insensible to these daily mercies.
Thy hand bestows blessings: thy power averts evil.
I bring my tribute of thanks for spiritual graces,
   the full warmth of faith,
   the cheering presence of thy Spirit,
   the strength of thy restraining will,
   thy spiking of hell's artillery.
Blessed be my sovereign Lord!

EVENING RENEWAL

MY FATHER,
If thy mercy had bounds, where would be my refuge from just wrath?
But thy love in Christ is without measure.
Thus, I present myself to thee
    with sins of commission and omission,
        against thee, my Father,
        against thee, adorable redeemer,
        against thee and thy strivings, O Holy Spirit,
        against the dictates of my conscience,
        against the precepts of thy Word,
        against my neighbours and myself.
Enter not into judgment with me,
For I plead no righteousness of my own,
  and have no cloak for iniquity.
Pardon my day dark with evil.
This night I renew my penitence.
Every morning I vow to love thee more fervently,
        to serve thee more sincerely,
        to be more devoted in my life,
        to be wholly thine;
Yet I soon stumble, backslide,
  and have to confess my weakness, misery and sin.
But I bless thee that the finished work of Jesus needs no addition
        from my doings,
     that his oblation is sufficient satisfaction
        for my sins.
If future days be mine, help me to amend my life,
        to hate and abhor evil,
        to flee the sins I confess.
Make me more resolute, more watchful, more prayerful.
Let no evil fruit spring from evil seeds my hands have sown;
Let no neighbour be hardened in vanity and folly
    by my want of circumspection.
If this day I have been ashamed of Christ and his Word,
    or have shown unkindness, malice, envy, lack of love,
    unadvised speech, hasty temper,

let it be no stumbling block to others,
or dishonour to thy name.
O help me to set an upright example that will ever rebuke vice,
allure to goodness,
and evidence that lovely are the ways of Christ.

V
Holy Aspirations

LONGINGS AFTER GOD

MY DEAR LORD,
I can but tell thee that thou knowest
    I long for nothing but thyself,
        nothing but holiness,
        nothing but union with thy will.
Thou hast given me these desires,
    and thou alone canst give me the thing desired.
My soul longs for communion with thee,
    for mortification of indwelling corruption,
        especially spiritual pride.
How precious it is
    to have a tender sense and clear apprehension
        of the mystery of godliness,
        of true holiness!
What a blessedness to be like thee
    as much as it is possible for a creature to be like its creator!
Lord, give me more of thy likeness;
Enlarge my soul to contain fullness of holiness;
Engage me to live more for thee.
Help me to be less pleased with my spiritual experiences,
    and when I feel at ease after sweet communings,
    teach me it is far too little I know and do.
Blessed Lord,
    let me climb up near to thee,
    and love, and long, and plead, and wrestle with thee,
    and pant for deliverance from the body of sin,
    for my heart is wandering and lifeless,
    and my soul mourns to think
        it should ever lose sight of its beloved.
Wrap my life in divine love,
    and keep me ever desiring thee,
always humble and resigned to thy will,
    more fixed on thyself,
    that I may be more fitted for doing and suffering.

CONSECRATION AND WORSHIP

MY GOD,
 I feel it is heaven to please thee,
 and to be what thou wouldst have me be.
O that I were holy as thou art holy,
   pure as Christ is pure,
   perfect as thy Spirit is perfect!
These, I feel, are the best commands in thy Book,
 and shall I break them? must I break them?
 am I under such a necessity as long as I live here?
Woe, woe is me that I am a sinner,
   that I grieve this blessed God,
   who is infinite in goodness and grace!
O, if he would punish me for my sins,
 it would not wound my heart so deep to offend him;
But though I sin continually,
 he continually repeats his kindness to me.
At times I feel I could bear any suffering,
 but how can I dishonour this glorious God?
What shall I do to glorify and worship this best of beings?
O that I could consecrate my soul and body to his service,
 without restraint, for ever!
O that I could give myself up to him,
   so as never more to attempt to be my own!
   or have any will or affections
    that are not perfectly conformed to his will
    and his love!
But, alas, I cannot live and not sin.
O may angels glorify him incessantly,
 and, if possible, prostrate themselves lower
 before the blessed king of heaven!
I long to bear a part with them in ceaseless praise;
But when I have done all I can to eternity
   I shall not be able to offer more than a small fraction
    of the homage that the glorious God deserves.
Give me a heart full of divine, heavenly love.

RESTING ON GOD

O GOD MOST HIGH, MOST GLORIOUS,
The thought of thine infinite serenity cheers me,
For I am toiling and moiling, troubled and distressed,
      but thou art for ever at perfect peace.
Thy designs cause thee no fear or care of unfulfilment,
      they stand fast as the eternal hills.
Thy power knows no bond,
      thy goodness no stint.
Thou bringest order out of confusion,
      and my defeats are thy victories:
The Lord God omnipotent reigneth.
I come to thee as a sinner with cares and sorrows,
      to leave every concern entirely to thee,
          every sin calling for Christ's precious blood;
Revive deep spirituality in my heart;
Let me live near to the great shepherd,
      hear his voice, know its tones, follow its calls.
Keep me from deception by causing me to abide in the truth,
      from harm by helping me to walk in the power of the Spirit.
Give me intenser faith in the eternal verities,
      burning into me by experience the things I know;
Let me never be ashamed of the truth of the gospel,
      that I may bear its reproach,
          vindicate it,
          see Jesus as its essence,
          know in it the power of the Spirit.
Lord, help me, for I am often lukewarm and chill;
      unbelief mars my confidence,
      sin makes me forget thee.
Let the weeds that grow in my soul be cut at their roots;
Grant me to know that I truly live only when I live to thee,
      that all else is trifling.
They presence alone can make me holy, devout, strong and happy.
Abide in me, gracious God.

DEVOTION

GOD OF MY END,
It is my greatest, noblest pleasure
        to be acquainted with thee
        and with my rational, immortal soul;
It is sweet and entertaining
        to look into my being
        when all my powers and passions
        are united and engaged in pursuit of thee,
        when my soul longs and passionately breathes
        after conformity to thee
        and the full enjoyment of thee;
No hours pass away with so much pleasure
        as those spent in communion with thee
        and with my heart.
O how desirable, how profitable to the Christian life
        is a spirit of holy watchfulness
        and godly jealousy over myself.
        when my soul is afraid of nothing
        except grieving and offending thee, the blessed God,
        my Father and friend,
        whom I then love and long to please,
        rather than be happy in myself!
Knowing, as I do, that this is *the* pious temper,
        worthy of the highest ambition, and closest pursuit
        of intelligent creatures and holy Christians,
        may my joy derive from glorifying and delighting thee.
I long to fill all my time for thee,
        whether at home or in the way;
        to place all my concerns in thy hands;
        to be entirely at thy disposal,
        having no will or interest of my own.
Help me to live to thee for ever,
        to make thee my last and only end,
        so that I may never more in one instance love my sinful self.

THE PERSONAL TOUCH

THOU GREAT *I AM*,
I acknowledge and confess that all things come of thee —
      life, breath, happiness, advancement,
      sight, touch, hearing,
      goodness, truth, beauty —
      all that makes existence amiable.
In the spiritual world also I am dependent entirely upon thee.
Give me grace to know more of my need of grace;
Show me my sinfulness that I may willingly confess it;
Reveal to me my weakness that I may know my strength in thee.
I thank thee for any sign of penitence; give me more of it;
My sins are black and deep,
      and rise from a stony, proud, self-righteous heart;
Help me to confess them with mourning, regret, self-loathing,
      with no pretence to merit or excuse;
I need healing,
Good physician, here is scope for thee,
      come and manifest thy power;
I need faith;
Thou who hast given it me, maintain, strengthen, increase it,
Centre it upon the Saviour's work,
      upon the majesty of the Father,
      upon the operations of the Spirit;
Work it in me now that I may never doubt thee
  as the truthful, mighty, faithful God.
Then I can bring my heart to thee
      full of love, gratitude, hope, joy.
May I lay at thy feet these fruits grown in thy garden,
      love thee with a passion that can never cool,
      believe in thee with a confidence that never staggers,
      hope in thee with an expectation that can never be dim,
      delight in thee with a rejoicing that cannot be stifled,
      glorify thee with the highest of my powers,
        burning, blazing, glowing, radiating, as from thy own glory.

DIVINE PROMISES

GLORIOUS JEHOVAH, MY COVENANT GOD,
All thy promises in Christ Jesus are yea and amen,
    and all shall be fulfilled.
Thou hast spoken them, and they shall be done,
    commanded, and they shall come to pass.
Yet I have often doubted them,
    have lived at times as if there were no God.
Lord, forgive me that death in life,
    when I have found something apart from thee,
    when I have been content with ephemeral things.
But through thy grace I have repented;
Thou hast given me to read my pardon in the wounds of Jesus,
    and my soul doth trust in him, my God incarnate,
    the ground of my life, the spring of my hope.
Teach me to be resigned to thy will,
    to delight in thy law,
    to have no will but thine,
    to believe that everything thou doest is for my good.
Help me to leave my concerns in thy hands,
    for thou hast power over evil,
    and bringest from it an infinite progression of good,
    until thy purposes are fulfilled.
Bless me with Abraham's faith
    that staggers not at promises through unbelief.
May I not instruct thee in my troubles,
    but glorify thee in my trials;
Grant me a distinct advance in the divine life;
    May I reach a higher platform,
    leave the mists of doubt and fear in the valley,
    and climb to hill-tops of eternal security in Christ
        by simply believing he cannot lie,
        or turn from his purpose.
Give me the confidence I ought to have in him
    who is worthy to be praised, and who is blessed for
    evermore.

SPIRITUAL HELPS

ETERNAL FATHER,
It is amazing love,
> that thou hast sent thy Son to suffer in my stead,
> that thou hast added the Spirit to teach, comfort, guide,
> that thou hast allowed the ministry of angels
> > to wall me round;

All heaven subserves the welfare of a poor worm.
Permit thy unseen servants to be ever active on my behalf,
> and to rejoice when grace expands in me.

Suffer them never to rest until my conflict is over,
> and I stand victorious on salvation's shore.

Grant that my proneness to evil, deadness to good,
> resistance to thy Spirit's motions,
> > may never provoke thee to abandon me.

May my hard heart awake thy pity, not thy wrath,
And if the enemy gets an advantage through my corruption,
> let it be seen that heaven is mightier than hell,
> that those for me are greater than those against me.

Arise to my help in richness of covenant blessings,
Keep me feeding in the pastures of thy strengthening Word,
> searching Scripture to find thee there.

If my waywardness is visited with a scourge,
> enable me to receive correction meekly,
> > to bless the reproving hand,
> > to discern the motive of rebuke,
> > to respond promptly, and do the first work.

Let all thy fatherly dealings make me a partaker of thy holiness.
Grant that in every fall I may sink lower on my knees,
> and that when I rise it may be to loftier heights of devotion.

May my every cross be sanctified,
> every loss be gain,
> every denial a spiritual advantage,
> every dark day a light of the Holy Spirit,
> every night of trial a song.

REFUGE

O LORD,

Whose power is infinite and wisdom infallible,
Order things that they may neither hinder, nor discourage me,
      nor prove obstacles to the progress of thy cause;
Stand between me and all strife, that no evil befall,
      no sin corrupt my gifts, zeal, attainments;
May I follow duty and not any foolish device of my own;
Permit me not to labour at work which thou wilt not bless,
      that I may serve thee without disgrace or debt;
Let me dwell in thy most secret place under thy shadow,
      where is safe impenetrable protection from
           the arrow that flieth by day,
           the pestilence that walketh in darkness,
           the strife of tongues,
           the malice of ill-will,
           the hurt of unkind talk,
           the snares of company,
           the perils of youth,
           the temptations of middle life,
           the mournings of old age,
           the fear of death.
I am entirely dependent upon thee for support, counsel, consolation.
Uphold me by thy free Spirit,
      and may I not think it enough to be preserved from falling,
      but may I always go forward,
      always abounding in the work thou givest me to do.
Strengthen me by thy Spirit in my inner self
      for every purpose of my Christian life.

All my jewels I give to the shadow of the safety that is in thee—
      my name anew in Christ,
      my body, soul, talents, character,
      my success, wife, children, friends, work,
      my present, my future, my end.
Take them, they are thine, and I am thine, now and for ever.

OPENNESS

LORD OF IMMORTALITY,
Before whom angels bow and archangels veil their faces,
 enable me to serve thee with reverence and godly fear.
Thou who art Spirit and requirest truth in the inward parts,
 help me to worship thee in spirit and in truth.
Thou who art righteous,
  let me not harbour sin in my heart,
    or indulge a worldly temper,
    or seek satisfaction in things that perish.
I hasten towards an hour
  when earthly pursuits and possessions will appear vain,
  when it will be indifferent whether I have been rich or poor,
  successful or disappointed,
  admired or despised.
But it will be of eternal moment that I have
mourned for sin,
   hungered and thirsted after righteousness,
   loved the Lord Jesus in sincerity,
   gloried in his cross.
May these objects engross my chief solicitude!
Produce in me those principles and dispositions
  that make thy service perfect freedom.
Expel from my mind all sinful fear and shame,
  so that with firmness and courage I may
    confess the redeemer before men,
    go forth with him bearing his reproach,
    be zealous with his knowledge,
    be filled with his wisdom,
    walk with his circumspection,
    ask counsel of him in all things,
    repair to the Scriptures for his orders,
    stay my mind on his peace,
   knowing that nothing can befall me
    without his permission, appointment and administration.

CHRISTLIKENESS

FATHER OF JESUS,
Dawn returns,
But without thy light within no outward light can profit;
Give me the saving lamp of thy Spirit that I may see thee,
      the God of my salvation, the delight of my soul,
      rejoicing over me in love.
I commend my heart to thy watchful care,
      for I know its treachery and power;
Guard its every portal from the wily enemy,
Give me quick discernment of his deadly arts,
Help me to recognize his bold disguise as an angel of light,
      and bid him begone.
May my words and works allure others to the highest walks
      of faith and love!
May loiterers be quickened to greater diligence by my example!
May worldlings be won to delight in acquaintance with thee!
May the timid and irresolute be warned of coming doom
      by my zeal for Jesus!
Cause me to be a mirror of thy grace,
      to show others the joy of thy service,
May my lips be well-tuned cymbals sounding thy praise,
Let a halo of heavenly-mindedness sparkle around me
      and a lamp of kindness sunbeam my path.
Teach me the happy art of attending to things temporal
      with a mind intent on things eternal.
Send me forth to have compasssion on the ignorant and miserable.
Help me to walk as Jesus walked,
      my only Saviour and perfect model,
      his mind my inward guest,
      his meekness my covering garb.
Let my happy place be amongst the poor in spirit,
      my delight the gentle ranks of the meek.
      Let me always esteem others better than myself,
      and find in true humility an heirdom to two worlds.

CHRISTIAN LOVE

O LOVER OF THE LOVELESS,
It is thy will that I should love thee
    with heart, soul, mind, strength,
    and my neighbour as myself.
But I am not sufficient for these things.
There is by nature no pure love in my soul;
Every affection in me is turned from thee;
I am bound, a slave to lust,
I cannot love thee, lovely as thou art,
    until thou dost set me free.
By grace I am thy freeman and would serve thee,
    for I believe thou art my God in Jesus,
    and that through him I am redeemed,
    and my sins are forgiven.
With this freedom I would always obey thee,
    but I cannot walk in liberty,
    any more than I could first attain it, of myself.
May thy Spirit draw me nearer to thee and thy ways.

Thou art the end of all means,
    for if they lead me not to thee,
    I go away empty.
Order all my ways by thy holy Word
    and make thy commandments the joy of my heart,
    that by them I may have happy converse with thee.
May I grow in thy love and manifest it to mankind.

Spirit of love, make me like the loving Jesus;
    give me his benevolent temper,
        his beneficent actions,
    that I may shine before men to thy glory.
The more thou doest in love in me and by me,
    humble me the more;
    keep me meek, lowly,
    and always ready to give thee honour.

LOVE SHED ABROAD

GRACIOUS GOD,
My heart praises thee for the wonder of thy love in Jesus;
He is heaven's darling, but is for me the incarnate,
  despised, rejected, crucified sin-bearer;
In him·thy grace has almost out-graced itself,
In him thy love to rebels has reached its height;
O to love thee with a love like this!
My heart is stone, melt it with thy love,
My heart is locked, let thy love be the master key to open it;
O Father, I adore thee for thy great love in the gift of Jesus,
O Jesus, I bless thee for resigning thy life for me,
O Holy Spirit, I thank thee for revealing to me this mystery;
Great God, let thy Son see in me the travail of his soul!
Bring me away from my false trusts to rest in him, and him only.
Let me not be so callous to his merit as not to love him,
  so indifferent to his blood as not to desire cleansing.
Lord Jesus, master, redeemer, saviour,
  come and take entire possession of me;
  this is thy right by purchase.
In the arms of love enfold and subdue my wilful spirit.
Take, sanctify, use my every faculty.
I am not ashamed of my hope,
  nor has my confidence led me into confusion.
I trusted in thee regarding my innumerable sins,
  and thou hast cast them behind thy back.
I trusted in thee when evils encompassed me,
  and thou broughtest me out into a wealthy place.
I trusted in thee in an hour of distress,
  and thou didst not fail me, though faith trembled.
O God of the eternal choice,
O God of the restored possession purchased on the tree,
O God of the effectual call,
Father, Son, Holy Spirit,
  I adore thy glory, honour, majesty, power, dominion
  for ever.

TO BE FIT FOR GOD

THOU MAKER AND SUSTAINER OF ALL THINGS,
Day and night are thine,
heaven and earth declare thy glory;
but I, a creature of thy power and bounty,
have sinned against thee
   by resisting the dictates of conscience,
     the demands of thy law,
     the calls of thy gospel;
  yet I live under the dispensation of a given hope.
Deliver me from worldly dispositions,
  for I am born from above and bound for glory.
May I view and long after holiness
  as the beauty and dignity of the soul.
Let me never slumber, never lose my assurance,
  never fail to wear armour when passing through enemy land.
Fit me for every scene and circumstance;
Stay my mind upon thee and turn my trials to blessings,
  that they may draw out my gratitude and praise
  as I see their design and effects.
Render my obedience to thy will holy, natural, and delightful.
Rectify all my principles by clear, consistent,
  and influential views of divine truth.
Let me never undervalue or neglect any part of thy revealed will.
May I duly regard the doctrine and practice of the gospel,
  prizing its commands as well as its promises.
Sanctify me in every relation, office, transaction
  and condition of life,
  that if I prosper I may not be unduly exalted,
   if I suffer I may not be over-sorrowful.
Balance my mind in all varying circumstances
  and help me to cultivate a disposition
  that renders every duty a spiritual privilege.
Thus may I be content, be a glory to thee
  and an example to others.

CONFIDENCE

O GOD, THOU ART VERY GREAT,
My lot is to approach thee with godly fear and humble confidence,
    for thy condescension equals thy grandeur,
    and thy goodness is thy glory.
I am unworthy, but thou dost welcome;
    guilty, but thou art merciful;
    indigent, but thy riches are unsearchable.
Thou hast shown boundless compassion towards me
    by not sparing thy Son,
    and by giving me freely all things in him;
This is the foundation of my hope,
    the refuge of my safety,
    the new and living way to thee,
    the means of that conviction of sin,
        brokenness of heart, and self-despair,
        which will endear to me the gospel.
Happy are they who are Christ's,
    in him at peace with thee,
      justified from all things,
      delivered from coming wrath,
      made heirs of future glory;
Give me such deadness to the world,
    such love to the Saviour,
    such attachment to his house,
    such devotedness to his service,
      as proves me a subject of his salvation.
May every part of my character and conduct
    make a serious and amiable impression on others,
    and impel them to ask the way to the master.
Let no incident of life, pleasing or painful,
    injure the prosperity of my soul, but rather increase it.
Send me thy help,
    for thine appointments are not meant to make me independent
      of thee,
    and the best means will be vain without super-added blessings.

COVENANT

LORD JESUS,
Grant me the favour of being led by thee,
        under the directions of thy providence and thy Word.
Grant me thy blessings with bitter things,
        to brighten and quicken me,
        not to depress and make me lifeless;
Grant me, like Gideon of old, way-tokens,
        by removing things that discourage me;
Grant me succour beneath the shadow of thy sympathy
        when I am tempted.
Accept my unceasing thanks
        that I am not cast off from thy hand
        as a darkened star or a rudderless vessel.
Suffer not my life to extend beyond my usefulness;
Cast me not under the feet of pride, injustice, riches,
        worldly greatness, selfish oppression of men;
Help me to wait patiently, silently upon thee,
        not to be enraged or speak unadvisedly.
Let thy mercy follow me while I live,
        and give me aid to resign myself to thy will.
Take my heart and hold it in thy hand;
        write upon it reverence to thyself
        with an inscription that time and eternity cannot erase.
To thy grace and the care of thy covenant
        I commit myself, in sickness, and in health,
        for thou hast overcome the world,
            fulfilled the law,
            finished justifying righteousness,
            swallowed up death in victory,
            and taken all power everywhere.
Mark this covenant with thine own blood
        in the court of forgiving mercy;
Attach unto it thy name in which I believe,
        for it is sealed by my unworthy mortal hand.

VI
Approach to God

ACT OF APPROACH

BENIGN LORD,
I praise thee continually
    for permission to approach thy throne of grace,
    and to spread my wants and desires before thee.
I am not worthy of thy blessings and mercies
    for I am far gone from original righteousness;
My depraved nature reveals itself in disobedience and rebellion;
My early days discovered in me discontent, pride, envy, revenge.
Remember not the sins of my youth,
      nor the multiplied transgressions of later years,
          my failure to improve time and talents,
          my abuse of mercies and means,
          my wasted sabbaths,
          my perverted seasons of grace,
          my long neglect of thy great salvation,
          my disregard of the friend of sinners.
While I confess my guilt, help me to feel it deeply,
    with self-abhorrence and self-despair, yet
    to remember there is hope in thee,
    and to see the Lamb that takes away sin.
Through him may I return to thee,
          listen to thee,
          trust in thee,
          delight in thy law,
          obey thee,
          be upheld by thee.
Preserve my understanding from error,
      my affections from love of idols,
      my lips from speaking guile,
      my conduct from stain of vice,
      my character from appearance of evil,
        that I may be harmless, blameless, rebukeless,
        exemplary, useful, light-giving, prudent, zealous for
          thy glory and the good of my fellow-men.

IN PRAYER

O LORD,
In prayer I launch far out into the eternal world,
      and on that broad ocean my soul triumphs
      over all evils on the shores of mortality.
Time, with its gay amusements and cruel disappointments
      never appears so inconsiderate as then.
In prayer I see myself as nothing;
      I find my heart going after thee with intensity,
      and long with vehement thirst to live to thee.
Blessed be the strong gales of the Spirit
      that speed me on my way to the New Jerusalem.
In prayer all things here below vanish,
      and nothing seems important
      but holiness of heart and the salvation of others.
In·prayer all my worldly cares, fears, anxieties disappear,
      and are of as little significance as a puff of wind.
In prayer my soul inwardly exults with lively thoughts
      at what thou art doing for thy church,
      and I long that thou shouldest get thyself a great name
      from sinners returning to Zion.
In prayer I am lifted above the frowns and flatteries of life,
      and taste heavenly joys;
      entering into the eternal world
      I can give myself to thee with all my heart,
      to be thine for ever.
In prayer I can place all my concerns in thy hands,
      to be entirely at thy disposal,
      having no will or interest of my own.
In prayer I can intercede for my friends, ministers,
      sinners, the church, thy kingdom to come,
      with greatest freedom, ardent hopes,
      as a son to his father,
      as a lover to the beloved.
Help me to be all prayer and never to cease praying.

LIVING BY PRAYER

O GOD OF THE OPEN EAR,
Teach me to live by prayer as well as by providence,
      for myself, soul, body, children, family, church;
Give me a heart frameable to thy will;
      so might I live in prayer,
      and honour thee,
      being kept from evil, known and unknown.
Help me to see the sin that accompanies all I do,
      and the good I can distil from everything.
Let me know that the work of prayer is to bring my will to thine,
      and that without this it is folly to pray;
When I try to bring thy will to mine it is to command Christ,
      to be above him, and wiser than he:
      this is my sin and pride.
I can only succeed when I pray
      according to thy precept and promise,
      and to be done with as it pleases thee,
      according to thy sovereign will.
When thou commandest me to pray for pardon, peace, brokenness,
      it is because thou wilt give me the thing promised,
      for thy glory, as well as for my good.
Help me not only to desire small things
      but with holy boldness to desire great things
      for thy people, for myself,
      that they and I might live to show thy glory.
Teach me that it is wisdom for me to pray for all I have,
      out of love, willingly, not of necessity;
      that I may come to thee at any time,
      to lay open my needs acceptably to thee;
      that my great sin lies in my not keeping the savour of thy
      ways;
      that the remembrance of this truth is one way
      to the sense of thy presence;
      that there is no wrath like the wrath of being governed
      by my own lusts for my own ends.

MEETING GOD

GREAT GOD,
In public and private, in sanctuary and home,
    may my life be steeped in prayer,
    filled with the spirit of grace and supplication,
    each prayer perfumed with the incense of atoning blood.
Help me, defend me, until from praying ground
I pass to the realm of unceasing praise.
Urged by my need,
Invited by thy promises,
Called by thy Spirit,
I enter thy presence, worshipping thee with godly fear,
          awed by thy majesty, greatness, glory,
          but encouraged by thy love.
I am all poverty as well as all guilt,
    having nothing of my own with which to repay thee,
But I bring Jesus to thee in the arms of faith,
    pleading his righteousness to offset my iniquities,
    rejoicing that he will weigh down the scales for me,
    and satisfy thy justice.
I bless thee that great sin draws out great grace,
      that, although the lest sin deserves infinite punishment
      because done against an infinite God,
      yet there is mercy for me,
      for where guilt is most terrible,
      there thy mercy in Christ is most free and deep.
Bless me by revealing to me more of his saving merits,
    by causing thy goodness to pass before me,
    by speaking peace to my contrite heart;
Strengthen me to give thee no rest
      until Christ shall reign supreme within me,
      in every thought, word, and deed,
      in a faith that purifies the heart,
          overcomes the world, works by love,
          fastens me to thee, and ever clings to
          the cross.

THE PRAYER OF LOVE

GRACIOUS LORD,
Thy name is love,
     in love receive my prayer.
My sins are more than the wide sea's sand,
     but where sin abounds, there is grace more abundant.
Look to the cross of thy beloved Son,
     and view the preciousness of his atoning blood;
Listen to his never-failing intercession,
     and whisper to my heart, 'Thy sins are forgiven,
     be of good cheer, lie down in peace.'
Grace cataracts from heaven and flows for ever,
     and mercy never wearies in bestowing benefits.
Grant me more and more
     to prize the privilege of prayer,
     to come to thee as a sin-soiled sinner,
     to find pardon in thee,
     to converse with thee;
     to know thee in prayer as
       the path in which my feet tread,
       the latch upon the door of my lips,
       the light that shines through my eyes,
       the music of my ears,
       the marrow of my understanding,
       the strength of my will,
       the power of my affection,
       the sweetness of my memory.
May the matter of my prayer be always wise, humble, submissive,
     obedient, scriptural, Christ-like.
Give me unwavering faith that supplications are never in vain,
     that if I seem not to obtain my petitions
     I shall have larger, richer answers,
     surpassing all that I ask or think.
Unsought, thou hast given me the greatest gift,
     the person of thy Son,
     and in him thou wilt give me all I need.

THE THRONE

O GOD OF MY DELIGHT,
Thy throne of grace is the pleasure ground of my soul.
      Here I obtain mercy in time of need,
      here see the smile of thy reconciled face,
      here joy pleads the name of Jesus,
      here I sharpen the sword of the Spirit,
            anoint the shield of faith,
            put on the helmet of salvation,
            gather manna from thy Word,
            am strengthened for each conflict,
                nerved for the upward race,
                empowered to conquer every foe;
Help me to come to Christ
      as the fountain head of descending blessings,
      as a wide open flood-gate of mercy.
I marvel at my insensate folly,
      that with such enriching favours within my reach
      I am slow to extend the hand to take them.
Have mercy upon my deadness for thy name's sake.
Quicken me, stir me, fill me with holy zeal.
Strengthen me that I may cling to thee and not let thee go.
May thy Spirit within me draw all blessings from thy hand.
When I advance not, I backslide.
Let me walk humbly because of good omitted and evil done.
Impress on my mind the shortness of time,
              the work to be engaged in,
              the account to be rendered,
              the nearness of eternity,
              the fearful sin of despising thy Spirit.
May I never forget that thy eye always sees,
          thy ear always hears,
          thy recording hand always writes.
May I never give thee rest until Christ is the pulse of my heart;
      the spokesman of my lips, the lamp of my feet.

REQUESTS

O GOD,
May I never be a blot or a blank in life,
   cause the way of truth to be evil spoken of,
   or make my liberty an occasion to the flesh.
May I by love serve others,
 and please my neighbour for his good to edification.
May I attend to what is ornamental as well as essential in religion,
 pursuing things that are lovely and of good report.
May I render my profession of the gospel not only impressive,
 but amiable and inviting.
May I hold forth the way of Jesus
 with my temper as well as my tongue,
 with my life as well as my lips.
May I say to all I meet,
 I am journeying towards the Lord's given place,
 come with me for your good.
May I be prepared
 for all the allotments of this short, changing, uncertain life,
 with a useful residence in it,
 a comfortable journey through it,
 a safe passage out of it.
May I be in character and conduct
 like the dew of heaven, the salt of the earth,
 the light of the world, the fullness of the fountain.
May I never be ashamed of Jesus or his words,
   never be deterred from fulfilling a known duty through fear,
   never be discouraged from attempting it through weakness.
May I see all things in a divine light so that they may
 inform my judgment and sanctify my heart.
And by all the disciplines of thy providence,
 and all the ordinances of religion,
 may I be increasingly prepared for life's remaining duties,
 the solemnities of a dying hour,
 and the joys and services that lie byond the grave.

AFTER PRAYER

O GOD OF GRACE,
I bewail my cold, listless, heartless prayers;
    their poverty adds sin to sin.
If my hope were in them I should be undone,
But the worth of Jesus perfumes my feeble breathings,
    and wins their acceptance.
Deepen my contrition of heart,
Confirm my faith in the blood that washes from all sin.
May I walk lovingly with my great redeemer.
Flood my soul with true repentance
    that my heart may be broken for sin and unto sin.
Let me be as slow to forgive myself as thou art ready to forgive me.
Gazing on the glories of thy grace
    may I be cast into the lowest depths of shame,
    and walk with downcast head
    now thou art pacified towards me.
O my great high priest,
    pour down upon me streams of needful grace,
    bless me in all my undertakings,
        in every thought of my mind,
          every word of my lips,
          every step of my feet.
          every deed of my hands.
Thou didst live to bless,
        die to bless,
        rise to bless,
        ascend to bless,
        take thy throne to bless, and
        now thou dost reign to bless.
O give sincerity to my desires,
    earnestness to my supplications,
    fervour to my love.

A COLLOQUY ON REJOICING

REMEMBER, O MY SOUL,
It is thy duty and privilege to rejoice in God:
He requires it of thee for all his favours of grace.
Rejoice then in the giver and his goodness,
Be happy in him, O my heart, and in nothing but God,
    for whatever a man trusts in,
    from that he expects happiness.

He who is the ground of thy faith
    should be the substance of thy joy.
Whence then come heaviness and dejection,
    when joy is sown in thee,
    promised by the Father,
    bestowed by the Son,
    inwrought by the Holy Spirit,
    thine by grace,
    thy birthright in believing?

Art thou seeking to rejoice in thyself
    from an evil motive of pride and self-reputation?
Thou hast nothing of thine own but sin,
      nothing to move God to be gracious,
      or to continue his grace towards thee.
If thou forget this thou wilt lose thy joy.
Art thou grieving under a sense of indwelling sin?
Let godly sorrow work repentance,
  as the true spirit which the Lord blesses,
  and which creates fullest joy;
Sorrow for self opens rejoicing in God,
Self-loathing draws down divine delights.
Hast thou sought joys in some creature comfort?
Look not below God for happiness;
  fall not asleep in Delilah's lap.
Let God be all in all to thee,
  and joy in the fountain that is always full.

VII
Gifts of Grace

GOD ALL-SUFFICIENT

O LORD OF GRACE,
The world is before me this day,
  and I am weak and fearful,
  but I look to thee for strength;
If I venture forth alone I stumble and fall,
  but on the beloved's arms I am firm as the eternal hills;
If left to the treachery of my heart I shall shame thy name,
  but if enlightened, guided, upheld by thy Spirit,
  I shall bring thee glory.
Be thou my arm to support,
   my strength to stand, my light to see,
   my feet to run, my shield to protect,
   my sword to repel, my sun to warm.
To enrich me will not diminish thy fullness;
All thy lovingkindness is in thy Son,
I bring him to thee in the arms of faith,
I urge his saving name as the one who died for me.
I plead his blood to pay my debts of wrong.
Accept his worthiness for my unworthiness,
  his sinlessness for my transgressions,
  his purity for my uncleanness,
  his sincerity for my guile,
  his truth for my deceits,
  his meekness for my pride,
  his constancy for my backslidings,
  his love for my enmity,
  his fullness for my emptiness,
  his faithfulness for my treachery,
  his obedience for my lawlessness,
  his glory for my shame,
  his devotedness for my waywardness,
  his holy life for my unchaste ways,
  his righteousness for my dead works,
  his death for my life.

PRIVILEGES

O LORD GOD,
Teach me to know that grace precedes, accompanies, and follows
                    my salvation,
              that it sustains the redeemed soul,
              that not one link of its chain can ever break.
From Calvary's cross wave upon wave of grace reaches me,
        deals with my sin,
        washes me clean,
        renews my heart,
        strengthens my will,
        draws out my affection,
        kindles a flame in my soul,
        rules throughout my inner man,
        consecrates my every thought, word, work,
        teaches me thy immeasurable love.
How great are my privileges in Christ Jesus!
Without him I stand far off, a stranger, an outcast;
      in him I draw near and touch his kingly sceptre.
Without him I dare not lift up my guilty eyes;
      in him I gaze upon my Father-God and friend.
Without him I hide my lips in trembling shame;
      in him I open my mouth in petition and praise.
Without him all is wrath and consuming fire;
      In him is all love, and the repose of my soul.
Without him is gaping hell below me, and eternal anguish;
      in him its gates are barred to me by his precious blood.
Without him darkness spreads its horrors in front;
      in him an eternity of glory is my boundless horizon.
Without him all within me is terror and dismay,
      in him every accusation is charmed into joy and peace.
Without him all things external call for my condemnation;
      in him they minister to my comfort,
      and are to be enjoyed with thanksgiving.
Praise be to thee for grace,
      and for the unspeakable gift of Jesus.

BLESSINGS

THOU GREAT THREE-ONE,
Author of all blessings I enjoy, of all I hope for,
Thou hast taught me
    that neither the experience of present evils,
    nor the remembrances of former sins,
    nor the remonstrances of friends,
    will or can affect a sinner's heart,
    except thou vouchsafe to reveal thy grace
    and quicken the dead in sin
    by the effectual working of thy Spirit's power.
Thou hast shown me
    that the sensible effusions of divine love in the soul
    are superior to and distinct from bodily health,
    and that oft-times spiritual comforts are at their highest
    when physical well-being is at its lowest.
Thou hast given me the ordinance of song as a means of grace;
Fit me to bear my part in that music ever new,
    which elect angels and saints made perfect
    now sing before thy·throne and before the Lamb.
I bless thee for tempering every distress with joy;
    too much of the former might weigh me down,
    too much of the latter might puff me up;
Thou art wise to give me a taste of both.
I love thee
    for giving me clusters of grapes in the wilderness,
    and drops of heavenly wine
    that set me longing to have my fill.
Apart from thee I quickly die,
    bereft of thee I starve,
    far from thee I thirst and droop;
But thou art all I need.
    Let me continually grasp the promise,
    'I will never leave thee nor forsake thee.'

FAITH

MY GOD,
I bless thee that thou hast given me the eye of faith,
      to see thee as Father,
      to know thee as a covenant God,
      to experience thy love planted in me;
For faith is the grace of union
      by which I spell out my entitlement to thee:
Faith casts my anchor upwards where I trust in thee
      and engage thee to be my Lord.
Be pleased to live and move within me,
      breathing in my prayers,
      inhabiting my praises,
      speaking in my words,
      moving in my actions,
      living in my life,
      causing me to grow in grace.
Thy bounteous goodness has helped me believe,
      but my faith is weak and wavering,
      its light dim,
      its steps tottering,
      its increase slow,
      its backslidings frequent;
It should scale the heavens but lies grovelling in the dust.
Lord, fan this divine spark into glowing flame.
When faith sleeps, my heart becomes an unclean thing,
      the fount of every loathsome desire,
      the cage of unclean lusts
      all fluttering to escape,
      the noxious tree of deadly fruit,
      the open wayside of earthly tares.
Lord, awake faith to put forth its strength
      until all heaven fills my soul
      and all impurity is cast out.

LOVE

LORD JESUS,
Give me to love thee, to embrace thee,
   though I once took lust and sin in my arms.
Thou didst love me before I loved thee,
   an enemy, a sinner, a loathsome worm.
Thou didst own me when I disclaimed myself;
Thou dost love me as a son,
   and weep over me as over Jerusalem.
Love brought thee from heaven to earth,
               from earth to the cross,
               from the cross to the grave.
Love caused thee to be weary, hungry, tempted,
   scorned, scourged, buffeted, spat upon, crucified, and pierced.
Love led thee to bow thy head in death.
My salvation is the point where perfect created love
   and the most perfect uncreated love meet together;
For thou dost welcome me, not like Joseph and his brothers,
   loving and sorrowing, but loving and rejoicing.
Thy love is not intermittent, cold, changeable;
   it does not cease or abate for all my enmity.

Holiness is a spark from thy love
   kindled to a flame in my heart by thy Spirit,
      and so it ever turns to the place from which it comes.
Let me see thy love everywhere, not only in the cross,
   but in the fellowship of believers and in the world around me.
When I feel the warmth of the sun may I praise thee
   who art the Sun of righteousness with healing power.
When I feel the tender rain
   may I think of the gospel showers that water my soul.
When I walk by the river side
   may I praise thee for that stream that makes the eternal city glad,
      and washes white my robes that I may have the right to the tree
        of life.
Thy infinite love is a mystery of mysteries,
   and my eternal rest lies in the eternal enjoyment of it.

JOY

O CHRIST,
All thy ways of mercy tend to and end in my delight.
Thou didst weep, sorrow, suffer that I might rejoice.
For my joy thou hast sent the Comforter,
                     multiplied thy promises,
                     shown me my future happiness,
                     given me a living fountain.
Thou art preparing joy for me and me for joy;
I pray for joy, wait for joy, long for joy;
   give me more than I can hold, desire, or think of.
Measure out to me my times and degrees of joy,
   at my work, business, duties.
If I weep at night, give me joy in the morning.
Let me rest in the thought of thy love,
                  pardon for sin, my title to heaven,
                  my future unspotted state.
I am an unworthy recipient of thy grace.
I often disesteem thy blood and slight thy love,
     but can in repentance draw water
     from the wells of thy joyous forgiveness.
Let my heart leap towards the eternal sabbath,
   where the work of redemption, sanctification,
   preservation, glorification
   is finished and perfected for ever,
   where thou wilt rejoice over me with joy.
There is no joy like the joy of heaven,
   for in that state are no sad divisions, unchristian quarrels,
   contentions, evil designs, weariness, hunger, cold,
   sadness, sin, suffering, persecutions, toils of duty.
O healthful place where none are sick!
O happy land where all are kings!
O holy assembly where all are priests!
How free a state where none are servants except to thee!
Bring me speedily to the land of joy.

CONTENTMENT

If I should suffer need, and go unclothed, and be in poverty,
  make my heart prize thy love, know it, be constrained by it,
  though I be denied all blessings.
It is thy mercy to afflict and try me with wants,
  for by these trials I see my sins,
  and desire severance from them.
Let me willingly accept misery, sorrows, temptations,
  if I can thereby feel sin as the greatest evil,
  and be delivered from it with gratitude to thee,
  acknowledging this as the highest testimony of thy love.
When thy Son, Jesus, came into my soul instead of sin
  he became more dear to me than sin had formerly been;
  his kindly rule replaced sin's tyranny.
Teach me to believe that if ever I would have any sin subdued
  I must not only labour to overcome it,
  but must invite Christ to abide in the place of it,
  and he must become to me more than vile lust had been;
  that his sweetness, power, life may be there.
Thus I must seek a grace from him contrary to sin,
  but must not claim it apart from himself.
When I am afraid of evils to come, comfort me by showing me
  that in myself I am a dying, condemned wretch,
    but in Christ I am reconciled and live;
  that in myself I find insufficiency and no rest,
    but in Christ there is satisfaction and peace;
  that in myself I am feeble and unable to do good,
    but in Christ I have ability to do all things.
Though now I have his graces in part,
  I shall shortly have them perfectly
  in that state where thou wilt show thyself fully reconciled,
  and alone sufficient, efficient, loving me completely,
  with sin abolished.
O Lord, hasten that day.

REPOSE

HEAVENLY FATHER,
My faith is in thee,
My expectation is from thee,
My love goes out toward thee.
    I believe thee,
      accept thy Word,
      acquiesce in thy will,
      rely on thy promises,
      trust thy providence.
I bless thee that the court of conscience
      proves me to be thine.
I do not need signs and wonders to believe,
      for thy Word is sure truth.
I have cast my anchor in the port of peace,
      knowing that present and future are in nail-pierced hands.
Thou art so good, wise, just, holy,
      that no mistake is possible to thee.
Thou art fountain and source of all law;
      what thou commandest is mine to obey.
I yield to thy sovereignty all that I am and have;
      do thou with me as thou wilt.
Thou hast given me silence in my heart
      in place of murmurings and complaints.
Keep my wishes from growing into willings,
      my willings from becoming fault-finding with thy providences,
      and have mercy·on me.
If I sin and am rebellious, help me to repent;
      then take away my mourning and give me music;
      remove my sackcloth and adorn me with beauty;
      take away my sighs and fill my mouth with songs;
      and when I am restored and rest in thee
      give me summer weather in my heart.

SLEEP

BLESSED CREATOR,
Thou hast promised thy beloved sleep;
Give me restoring rest needful for tomorrow's toil.
If dreams be mine, let them not be tinged with evil.
Let thy Spirit make my time of repose a blessed temple of his holy
    presence.

May my frequent lying down make me familiar with death,
    the bed I approach remind me of the grave,
    the eyes I now close picture to me their final closing.
Keep me always ready, waiting for admittance to thy presence.
Weaken my attachment to earthly things.
May I hold life loosely in my hand,
    knowing that I receive it on condition of its surrender;
As pain and suffering betoken transitory health,
    may I not shrink from a death
    that introduces me to the freshness of eternal youth.
I retire this night in full assurance of one day awaking with thee.
All glory for this precious hope,
    for the gospel of grace,
    for thine unspeakable gift of Jesus,
    for the fellowship of the Trinity.
Withhold not thy mercies in the night season;
    thy hand never wearies,
    thy power needs no repose,
    thine eye never sleeps.

Help me when I helpless lie,
    when my conscience accuses me of sin,
    when my mind is harassed by foreboding thoughts,
    when my eyes are held awake by personal anxieties.

Show thyself to me as the God of all grace, love and power;
    thou hast a balm for every wound,
    a solace for all anguish,
    a remedy for every pain,
    a peace for all disquietude.
Permit me to commit myself to thee awake or asleep.

COMFORTS

GIVER OF ALL GOOD,
Streams upon streams of love overflow my path.
Thou hast made me out of nothing,
    hast recalled me from a far country,
    hast translated me from ignorance to knowledge,
            from darkness to light,
            from death to life,
            from misery to peace,
            from folly to wisdom,
            from error to truth,
            from sin to victory.
Thanks be to thee for my high and holy calling.
I bless thee for ministering angels,
      for the comfort of thy Word,
      for the ordinances of thy church,
      for the teaching of thy Spirit,
      for thy holy sacraments,
      for the communion of saints,
      for Christian fellowship,
      for the recorded annals of holy lives,
      for examples sweet to allure,
      for beacons sad to deter.
Thy will is in all thy provisions
        to enable me to grow in grace,
        and to be meet for thy eternal presence.
My heaven-born faith gives promise of eternal sight,
      my new birth a pledge of never-ending life.
I draw near to thee, knowing thou wilt draw near to me.
I ask of thee, believing thou hast already given.
I entrust myself to thee, for thou hast redeemed me.
I bless and adore thee, the eternal God,
      for the comfort of these thoughts,
        the joy of these hopes.

FULLNESS

HEAVENLY FATHER,
Thou hast revealed to me myself as a mass of sin,
   and thyself as the fullness of goodness,
      with strength enough to succour me,
         wisdom enough to guide me,
         mercy enough to quicken me,
         love enough to satisfy me.
Thou hast shown me that because thou art mine
   I can live by thy life,
      be strong in thy strength,
      be guided by thy wisdom;
   and so I can pitch my thoughts and heart in thee.
This is the exchange of wonderful love—
   for me to have thee for myself,
   and for thee to have me, and to give me thyself.
There is in thee all fullness of the good I need,
   and the fullness of all grace to draw me to thyself,
      who else could never have come.
But having come, I must cleave to thee,
            be knit to thee,
            always seek thee.
There is none all good as thou art:
With thee I can live without other things,
   for thou art God all-sufficient,
   and the glory, peace, rest, joy of the world
   is a creaturely, perishing thing in comparison with thee.
Help me to know that he who hopes for nothing but thee,
   and for all things only for thee, hopes truly,
   and that I must place all my happiness in holiness,
   if I hope to be filled with all grace.
Convince me that I can have no peace at death,
   nor hope that I should go to Christ,
   unless I intend to do his will
   and have his fullness while I live.

HAPPINESS

O LORD,
Help me never to expect any happiness from the world,
    but only in thee.
Let me not think that I shall be more happy by living to myself,
    for I can only be happy if employed for thee,
    and if I desire to live in this world
    only to do and suffer what thou dost allot me.
Teach me
    that if I do not live a life that satisfies thee,
    I shall not live a life that will satisfy myself.
Help me to desire the spirit and temper of angels
    who willingly come down to this lower world
      to perform thy will,
    though their desires are heavenly,
    and not set in the least upon earthly things;
      then I shall be of that temper I ought to have.
Help me not to think of living to thee in my own strength,
    but always to look to and rely on thee for assistance.
Teach me that there is no greater truth than this,
    that I can do nothing of myself.
Lord, this is the life that no unconverted man can live,
    yet it is an end that every godly soul presses after;
Let it be then my concern to devote myself and all to thee.
Make me more fruitful and more spiritual,
    for barrenness is my daily affliction and load.
How precious is time, and how painful to see it fly
    with little done to good purpose!
I need thy help:
O may my soul sensibly depend upon thee
    for all sanctification,
    and every accomplishment of thy purposes
      for me, for the world,
      and for thy kingdom.

VOCATION

HEAVENLY FATHER,
Thou hast placed me in the church
    which thy Son purchased by his own blood.
Add grace to grace that I may live worthy of my vocation.

I am a voyager across life's ocean;
Safe in heaven's ark, may I pass through a troubled world
    into the harbour of eternal rest.

I am a tree of the vineyard thou hast planted.
Grant me not to be barren, with worthless leaves and wild **grapes**;
Prune me of useless branches;
Water me with dews of blessing.
I am part of the Lamb's bride, the church.
Help me to be true, faithful, chaste, loving, pure, devoted;
Let no strong affection wantonly dally with the world.
May I live high above a love of things temporal,
    sanctified, cleansed, unblemished, hallowed by grace,
    thy love my fullness,
    thy glory my joy,
    thy precepts my pathway,
    thy cross my resting place.
My heart is not always a flame of adoring love,
But, resting in thy Son's redemption,
    I look forward to the days of heaven,
      where no langour shall oppress,
          no iniquities chill,
          no mists of unbelief dim the eye,
          no zeal ever tires.
Father, these thoughts are the stay, prop, and comfort of my soul.

TRUTH IN JESUS

LIFE-GIVING GOD,
Quicken me to call upon thy name,
 for my mind is ignorant,
  my thoughts vagrant,
  my affections earthly,
  my heart unbelieving,
 and only thy Spirit can help my infirmities.
I approach thee as Father and friend,
 my portion for ever,
 my exceeding joy,
 my strength of heart.
I believe in thee as the God of nature,
   the ordainer of providence,
    the sender of Jesus my saviour.
My guilty fears discourage an approach to thee,
 but I praise thee for the blessed news
 that Jesus reconciles thee to me.
May the truth that is in him
 illuminate in me all that is dark,
 establish in me all that is wavering,
 comfort in me all that is wretched,
 accomplish in me all that is of thy goodness,
 and glorify in me the name of Jesus.
I pass through a vale of tears
 but bless thee for the opening gate of glory at its end.
Enable me to realize as mine the better, heavenly country.
Prepare me for every part of my pilgrimage.
Uphold my steps by thy Word.
Let no iniquity dominate me.
Teach me that Christ cannot be the way if I am the end,
  that he cannot be redeemer if I am my own saviour,
  that there can be no true union with him
   while the creature has my heart,
  that faith accepts him as redeemer and Lord or not at all.

GRACE IN TRIALS

FATHER OF MERCIES,
Hear me for Jesus' sake.
I am sinful even in my closest walk with thee;
    it is of thy mercy I died not long ago;
Thy grace has given me faith in the cross
    by which thou hast reconciled thyself to me
      ard me to thee,
    drawing me by thy great love,
    reckoning me as innocent in Christ though guilty in myself.
Giver of all graces,
    I look to thee for strength to maintain them in me,
    for it is hard to practise what I believe.
Strengthen me against temptations.
My heart is an unexhausted fountain of sin,
        a river of corruption since childhood days,
          flowing on in every pattern of behaviour;
Thou hast disarmed me of the means in which I trusted,
    and I have no strength but in thee.
Thou alone canst hold back my evil ways,
    but without thy grace to sustain me I fall.
Satan's darts quickly inflame me,
    and the shield that should quench them
      easily drops from my hand:
Empower me against his wiles and assaults.
Keep me sensible of my weakness,
    and of my dependence upon thy strength.
Let every trial teach me more of thy peace,
          more of thy love.
Thy Holy Spirit is given to increase thy graces,
    and I cannot preserve or improve them
    unless he works continually in me.
May he confirm my trust in thy promised help,
    and let me walk humbly in dependence upon thee,
      for Jesus' sake.

THE GRACE OF THE CROSS

O MY SAVIOUR,
I thank thee from the depths of my being
    for thy wondrous grace and love
    in bearing my sin in thine own body on the tree.
May thy cross be to me
        as the tree that sweetens my bitter Marahs,
        as the rod that blossoms with life and beauty,
        as the brazen serpent that calls forth the look of faith.
By thy cross crucify my every sin;
Use it to increase my intimacy with thyself;
Make it the ground of all my comfort,
      the liveliness of all my duties,
      the sum of all thy gospel promises,
      the comfort of all my afflictions,
      the vigour of my love, thankfulness, graces,
      the very essence of my religion;
And by it give me that rest without rest,
    the rest of ceaseless praise.

O MY LORD AND SAVIOUR,
Thou hast also appointed a cross for me to take up and carry,
    a cross before thou givest me a crown.
Thou hast appointed it to be my portion,
    but self-love hates it,
    carnal reason is unreconciled to it;
    without the grace of patience I cannot bear it,
      walk with it, profit by it.
O blessed cross, what mercies dost thou bring with thee!
Thou art only esteemed hateful by my rebel will,
    heavy because I shirk thy load.
Teach me, gracious Lord and Saviour,
    that with my cross thou sendest promised grace
    so that I may bear it patiently,
    that my cross is thy yoke which is easy,
    and thy burden which is light.

CALVARY'S ANTHEM

HEAVENLY FATHER,
Thou hast led me singing to the cross
    where I fling down all my burdens and see them vanish,
    where my mountains of guilt are levelled to a plain,
where my sins disappear, though they are the greatest that exist,
    and are more in number than the grains of fine sand;

For there is power in the blood of Calvary
    to destroy sins more than can be counted
    even by one from the choir of heaven.
Thou hast given me a hill-side spring
    that washes clear and white,
    and I go as a sinner to its waters,
    bathing without hindrance in its crystal streams.
At the cross there is free forgiveness for poor and meek ones,
    and ample blessings that last for ever;
The blood of the Lamb is like a great river of infinite grace
    with never any diminishing of its fullness
    as thirsty ones without number drink of it.

O Lord, for ever will thy free forgiveness live
    that was gained on the mount of blood;
In the midst of a world of pain
    it is a subject for praise in every place
    a song on earth, an anthem in heaven,
    its love and virtue knowing no end.
I have a longing for the world above
    where multitudes sing the great song,
    for my soul was never created to love the dust of earth.
Though here my spiritual state is frail and poor,
    I shall go on singing Calvary's anthem.
May I always know
    that a clean heart full of goodness
        is more beautiful than the lily,
    that only a clean heart can sing by night and by day,
    that such a heart is mine when I abide at Calvary.

SINCERITY

ELECTOR OF SAINTS,
Blessed is the man whom thou choosest and callest to thyself.
With thee is mercy, redemption, assurance, forgiveness;
Thou hast lifted me, a prisoner, out of the pit of sin
    and pronounced my discharge,
        not only in the courts of heaven,
      but in the dock of conscience;
      hast justified me by faith,
          given me peace with thee,
           made me to enjoy glorious liberty as thy child.
Save me from the false hope of the hypocrite:
May I never suppose I am in Christ unless I am a new creature,
      never think I am born of the Spirit
         unless I mind the things of the Spirit,
       never rest satisfied with professions of belief
          and outward forms and services,
            while my heart is not right with thee.
May I judge my sincerity in religion
         by my fear to offend thee,
            my concern to know thy will,
            my willingness to deny myself.
May nothing render me forgetful of thy glory,
    or turn me aside from thy commands,
    or shake my confidence in thy promises,
    or offend thy children.
Let not my temporal occupations injure my spiritual concerns,
    or the cares of life make me neglect the one thing needful.
May I not be inattentive to the design of thy dealings with me,
    or insensible under thy rebukes,
    or immobile at thy calls.
May I learn the holy art of abiding in thee,
    of being in the world and not of it,
    of making everything not only consistent with
      but conducive to my religion.

VIII
Service and Ministry

GOD'S CAUSE

SOVEREIGN GOD,
Thy cause, not my own, engages my heart,
    and I appeal to thee with greatest freedom
    to set up thy kingdom in every place where Satan reigns;
Glorify thyself and I shall rejoice,
    for to bring honour to thy name is my sole desire.
I adore thee that thou art God,
    and long that others should know it, feel it,
      and rejoice in it.
O that all men might love and praise thee,
    that thou mightest have all glory from the intelligent world!
Let sinners be brought to thee for thy dear name!
To the eye of reason everything respecting the conversion of others
    is as dark as midnight,
But thou canst accomplish great things;
    the cause is thine,
    and it is to thy glory that men should be saved.
Lord, use me as thou wilt,
    do with me what thou wilt;
    but, O, promote thy cause,
    let thy kingdom come,
    let thy blessed interest be advanced in this world!
O do thou bring in great numbers to Jesus!
    let me see that glorious day,
      and give me to grasp for multitudes of souls;
    let me be willing to die to that end;
      and while I live let me labour for thee
        to the utmost of my strength,
        spending time profitably in this work,
        both in health and in weakness.
It is thy cause and kingdom I long for, not my own.

O, answer thou my request!

SERVICE AND EQUIPMENT

THOU GOD OF MY END,
Thou hast given me a fixed disposition
    to go forth and spend my life for thee;
If it be thy will let me proceed in it;
    if not, then revoke my intentions.
All I want in life is such circumstances
    as may best enable me to serve thee in the world;
To this end I leave all my concerns in thy hand,
    but let me not be discouraged,
    for this hinders my spiritual fervency;
Enable me to undertake some task for thee,
    for this refreshes and animates my soul,
    so that I could endure all hardships and labours,
    and willingly suffer for thy name.
But, O what a death it is to strive and labour,
    to be always in a hurry and yet do nothing!
Alas, time flies and I am of little use.
O that I could be a flame of fire in thy service,
    always burning out in one continual blaze.
Fit me for singular usefulness in this world.
Fit me to exult in distresses of every kind
    if they but promote the advancement of thy kingdom.
Fit me to quit all hopes of the world's friendship,
    and give me a deeper sense of my sinfulness.
Fit me to accept as just desert from thee
    any trial that may befall me.
Fit me to be totally resigned to the denial of pleasures I desire,
    and to be content to spend my time with thee.
Fit me to pray with a sense of the joy of divine communion,
    to find all times happy seasons to my soul,
    to see my own nothingness,
    and wonder that I am allowed to serve thee.
Fit me to enter the blessed world where no unclean thing is,
    and to know thee with me always.

THINGS NEEDFUL

THOU ETERNAL SOURCE,
Author of all created being and happiness,
I adore thee for making man capable of religion,
    that he may be taught to say:
      'Where is God my maker, who giveth songs in the night?'
But degeneracy has spread over our human race,
    turning glory into shame,
    rendering us forgetful of thee.
We know it is thy power alone
    that can recall wandering children,
    can impress on them a sense of divine things,
    and can render that sense lasting and effectual;
From thee proceed all good purposes and desires,
    and the diffusing of piety and happiness.
Thou hast knowledge of my soul's secret principles,
    and art aware of my desire to spread the gospel.
Make me an almoner to give thy
    bounties to the indigent,
    comfort to the mentally ill,
    restoration to the sin-diseased,
    hope to the despairing,
    joy to the sorrowing,
    love to the prodigals.
Blow away the ashes of unbelief by thy Spirit's breath
    and give me light, fire, and warmth of love.
I need spiritual comforts
    that are gentle, peaceful, mild, refreshing,
    that will melt me into conscious lowliness before thee,
    that will make me feel and rest in thee as my All.

Fill the garden of my soul with the wind of love,
    that the scents of the Christian life may be wafted to others;
    then come and gather fruits to thy glory.
So shall I fulfil the great end of my being—
    to glorify thee and be a blessing to men.

HUMILITY IN SERVICE

MIGHTY GOD,
I humble myself for faculties misused,
                          opportunities neglected,
                          words ill-advised,
I repent of my folly and inconsiderate ways,
            my broken resolutions, untrue service,
            my backsliding steps,
            my vain thoughts.
O bury my sins in the ocean of Jesus' blood
      and let no evil result from my fretful temper,
      unseemly behaviour, provoking pettiness.
If by unkindness I have wounded or hurt another,
      do thou pour in the balm of heavenly consolation;
If I have turned coldly from need, misery, grief,
      do not in just anger forsake me;
If I have withheld relief from penury and pain,
      do not withhold thy gracious bounty from me.
If I have shunned those who have offended me,
      keep open the door of thy heart to my need.

Fill me with an over-flowing ocean of compassion,
      the reign of love my motive,
      the law of love my rule.

O thou God of all grace, make me more thankful, more humble;
Inspire me with a deep sense of my unworthiness arising from
      the depravity of my nature, my omitted duties,
      my unimproved advantages, thy commands violated by me.
With all my calls to gratitude and joy may I remember
      that I have reason for sorrow and humiliation;
O give me repentance unto life;
Cement my oneness with my blessed Lord,
        that faith may adhere to him more immovably,
        that love may entwine itself round him more tightly,
        that his spirit may pervade every fibre of my being.
Then send me out to make him known to my fellow-men.

THE SERVANT IN BATTLE

O LORD,
I bless thee that the issue of the battle between thyself and Satan
       has never been uncertain,
       and will end in victory.
Calvary broke the dragon's head,
       and I contend with a vanquished foe,
       who with all his subtlety and strength
       has already been overcome.
When I feel the serpent at my heel
       may I remember him whose heel was bruised,
       but who, when bruised, broke the devil's head.

My soul with inward joy extols the mighty conqueror.

Heal me of any wounds received in the great conflict;
       if I have gathered defilement,
       if my faith has suffered damage,
       if my hope is less than bright,
       if my love is not fervent,
       if some creature-comfort occupies my heart,
       if my soul sinks under pressure of the fight.
O thou whose every promise is balm,
          every touch life,
       draw near to thy weary warrior,
       refresh me, that I may rise again to wage the strife,
       and never tire until my enemy is trodden down.
Give me such fellowship with thee that I may defy Satan,
       unbelief, the flesh, the world,
       with delight that comes not from a creature,
       and which a creature cannot mar.
Give me a draught of the eternal fountain
       that lieth in thy immutable, everlasting love and decree.
Then shall my hand never weaken, my feet never stumble,
       my sword never rest, my shield never rust,
       my helmet never shatter, my breastplate never fall,
       as my strength rests in the power of thy might.

VAIN SERVICE

O MY LORD,
Forgive me for serving thee in sinful ways –
   by glorying in my own strength,
   by forcing myself to minister through necessity,
   by accepting the applause of others,
   by trusting in assumed grace and spiritual affection,
   by a faith that rests upon my hold on Christ, not on him
    alone.
   by having another foundation to stand upon beside thee;
    for thus I make flesh my arm.
Help me to see
  that it is faith stirred by grace that does the deed,
  that faith brings a man nearer to thee,
   raising him above mere man,
  that thou dost act upon the soul when thus elevated
   and lifted out of itself,
  that faith centres in thee as God all-sufficient,
    Father, Son, Holy Spirit,
    as God efficient,
    mediately, as in thy commands and promises,
    immediately, in all the hidden power
     that faith sees and knows to be in thee,
    abundantly, with omnipotent effect,
     in the revelation of thy will.
If I have not such faith I am nothing.

It is my duty to set thee above all others in mind and eye;
But it is my sin that I place myself above thee.
Lord, it is the special evil of sin
    that every breach of thy law arises
     from contempt of thy person,
     from despising thee and thy glory,
     from preferring things before thee.
Help me to abhor myself in comparison of thee,
And keep me in a faith that works by love, and serves by grace.

LOVE REST IN GOD

MY DEAR LORD,
I depend wholly upon thee,
    wean me from all other dependences.
Thou art my all, thou dost overrule all and delight in me.
Thou art the foundation of goodness,
    how can I distrust thee?
    how be anxious about what happens to me?
In the light of thy preciousness
    the world and all its enjoyments are infinitely poor:
I value the favour of men no more than pebbles.
Amid the blessings I receive from thee
    may I never lose the heart of a stranger.
May I love thee, my benefactor, in all my benefits,
    not forgetting that my greatest danger
    arises from my advantages.
Produce in me self-despair that will make Jesus precious to me,
    delightful in all his offices,
    pleasureable in all his ways,
    and may I love his commands as well as his promises.
Help me to discern between true and false love,
    the one consisting of supreme love to thee, the other not,
    the former uniting thy glory and man·s happiness
        that they may become one common interest,
    the latter disjointing and separating them both,
        seeking the latter with neglect of the former.
Teach me that genuine love is different in kind
    from that wrought by rational arguments or the motive of
    self-interest,
    that such love is a pleasing passion affording joy to the mind
    where it is.
Grant me grace to distinguish between the genuine and the false,
    and to rest in thee who art all love.

A DISCIPLE'S RENEWAL

O MY SAVIOUR,
      help me.
I am so slow to learn, so prone to forget, so weak to climb;
I am in the foothills when I should be on the heights;
I am pained by my graceless heart,
               my prayerless days,
               my poverty of love,
               my sloth in the heavenly race,
               my sullied conscience,
               my wasted hours,
               my unspent opportunities.
I am blind while light shines around me:
      take the scales from my eyes,
      grind to dust the evil heart of unbelief.
Make it my chiefest joy to study thee,
                 meditate on thee,
                 gaze on thee,
                 sit like Mary at thy feet,
                 lean like John on thy breast,
                 appeal like Peter to thy love,
                 count like Paul all things dung.
Give me increase and progress in grace so that there may be
      more decision in my character,
      more vigour in my purposes,
      more elevation in my life,
      more fervour in my devotion,
      more constancy in my zeal.
As I have a position in the world,
      keep me from making the world my position;
May I never seek in the creature
      what can be found only in the creator;
Let not faith cease from seeking thee until it vanishes into sight.
Ride forth in me, thou king of kings and lord of lords,
      that I may live victoriously, and in victory attain my end.

A MINISTER'S EVILS

BLESSED SPIRIT OF GOD,
Four evils attend my ministry—
   The devil treads me down by discouragement and shame
      arising from coldness in private meditation.
   Carelessness possesses me
      from natural dullness and dimness of spirit;
      because in the past I have met with success
      and been highly regarded,
      so that it does not matter if I have now failed.
   Infirmities and weakness are mine from want of spiritual light,
         life and power,
      so that souls have not been helped,
      and I have not felt thee to be near.
   Lack of success has followed even when I have done my best.

But thou hast shown me that the glory of everything
      that is sanctified to do good
      is not seen in itself,
      but in the source of its sanctification.
Thus my end in preaching is to know Christ,
      and impart his truth;
      my principle in preaching is Christ himself, whom I trust,
      for in him is fullness of spirit and strength;
      my comfort in preaching is to do all for him.
Help me in my work to grow more humble,
      to pick something out of all providences to that end,
      to joy in thee and loathe myself,
      to keep my life, being, soul, and body only for thee,
      to carry my heart to thee in love and delight,
      to see all my grace in thee, coming from thee,
      to walk with thee in endearment.
Then, whether I succeed or fail, nought matters but thee alone.

A MINISTER'S PRAYER

O MY LORD,
Let not my ministry be approved only by men,
    or merely win the esteem and affections of people;
But do the work of grace in their hearts,
    call in thy elect,
    seal and edify the regenerate ones,
    and command eternal blessings on their souls.
Save me from self-opinion and self-seeking;
Water the hearts of those who hear thy Word,
    that seed sown in weakness may be raised in power;
Cause me and those that hear me
    to behold thee here in the light of special faith,
    and hereafter in the blaze of endless glory;
Make my every sermon a means of grace to myself,
    and help me to experience the power of thy dying love,
    for thy blood is balm,
    thy presence bliss,
    thy smile heaven,
    thy cross the place where truth and mercy meet.
Look upon the doubts and discouragements of my ministry
    and keep me from self-importance;
I beg pardon for my many sins, omissions, infirmities,
    as a man, as a minister;
Command thy blessing on my weak, unworthy labours,
    and on the message of salvation given;
Stay with thy people,
    and may thy presence be their portion and mine.
When I preach to others let not my words be merely elegant and
  masterly,
    my reasoning polished and refined,
    my performance powerless and tasteless,
    but may I exalt thee and humble sinners.
O Lord of power and grace,
    all hearts are in thy hands, all events at thy disposal,
    set the seal of thy almighty will upon my ministry.

A MINISTER'S CONFESSION

O GOD,
I know that I often do thy work without thy power,
  and sin by my dead, heartless, blind service,
    my lack of inward light, love, delight,
     my mind, heart, tongue moving without thy help.
I see sin in my heart in seeking the approbation of others;
This is my vileness, to make men's opinion my rule, whereas
  I should see what good I have done,
   and give thee glory,
  consider what sin I have committed and mourn for that.
It is my deceit to preach, and pray,
  and to stir up others' spiritual affections
  in order to beget commendations,
  whereas my rule should be daily to consider myself more vile
   than any man in my own eyes.
But thou dost show thy power by my frailty,
  so that the more feeble I am, the more fit to be used,
  for thou dost pitch a tent of grace in my weakness.
Help me to rejoice in my infirmities and give thee praise,
  to acknowledge my deficiencies before others
  and not be discouraged by them,
  that they may see thy glory more clearly.
Teach me that I must act by a power supernatural,
  whereby I can attempt things above my strength,
  and bear evils beyond my strength,
  acting for Christ in all, and
  having his superior power to help me.
Let me learn of Paul
  whose presence was mean,
  his weakness great,
  his utterance contemptible,
  yet thou didst account him faithful and blessed.
Lord, let me lean on thee as he did,
  and find my ministry thine.

A MINISTER'S STRENGTH

UNCHANGEABLE JEHOVAH,
When I am discouraged in my ministry
    and full of doubts of my self,
      fasten me upon the rock of thy eternal election,
      then my hands will not hang down,
      and I shall have hope for myself and others.
Thou dost know thy people by name,
      and wilt at the appointed season
        lead them out of a natural to a gracious state
      by thy effectual calling.
This is the ground of my salvation,
      the object of my desire,
      the motive of my ministry.
Keep me from high thoughts of myself or my work,
      for I am nothing but sin and weakness;
      in me no good dwells,
      and my best works are but sin.
Humble me to the dust before thee.
Root and tear out the poisonous weed of self-righteousness,
      and show me my utter nothingness;
Keep me sensible of my sinnership;
Sink me deeper into penitence and self-abhorrence;
Break the Dagon of pride in pieces before the ark of thy presence;
Demolish the Babel of self-opinion, and scatter it to the wind;
Level to the ground my Jericho walls of a rebel heart;
Then grace, grace, will be my experience and cry.
I am a poor, feeble creature when faith is not in exercise,
      like an eagle with pinioned wings;
Grant me to rest on thy power and faithfulness,
      and to know that there are two things worth living for:
      to further thy cause in the world,
      and to do good to the souls and bodies of men;
This is my ministry, my life, my prayer, my end.
Grant me grace that I shall not fail.

A MINISTER'S PRAISES

O GOD, MY EXCEEDING JOY,
Singing thy praises uplifts my heart,
  for thou art a fountain of delight,
  and dost bless the soul that joys in thee.
But because of my heart's rebellion
  I cannot always praise thee as I ought;
Yet I will at all times rest myself
  in thy excellences, goodness, and loving-kindness.
Thou art in Jesus the object of inexpressible joy,
  and I take exceeding pleasure in the thought of thee.
But, Lord, I am sometimes thy enemy;
  my nature revolts and wanders from thee.
Though thou hast renewed me,
  yet evil corruptions urge me still to oppose thee.
Help me to extol thee with entire heart-submission,
  to be diligent in self-examination,
  to ask myself
   whether I am truly born again,
   whether my spirit is the spirit of thy children,
   whether my griefs are those that tear repenting hearts,
   whether my joys are the joys of faith,
   whether my confidence in Christ works by love
   and purifies the soul.
Give me the sweet results of faith,
  in my secret character, and in my public life.
Cast cords of love around my heart,
  then hold me and never let me go.
May the saviour's wounds sway me more than the sceptre of princes.
Let me love thee in a love that covers and swallows up all,
  that I may not violate my chaste union with the beloved;
There is much unconquered territory in my nature,
  scourge out the buyers and sellers of my soul's temple,
  and give me in return pure desires,
  and longings after perfect holiness.

O GOD OF TRUTH,
I thank thee for the holy Scriptures,
  their precepts, promises, directions, light.
In them may I learn more of Christ,
  be enabled to retain his truth
  and have grace to follow it.
Help me to lift up the gates of my soul that he may come in
  and show me himself when I search the Scriptures,
  for I have no lines to fathom its depths,
  no wings to soar to its heights.
By his aid may I be enabled to explore all its truths,
  love them with all my heart,
  embrace them with all my power,
  engraft them into my life.
Bless to my soul all grains of truth garnered from thy Word;
  may they take deep root,
  be refreshed by heavenly dew,
  be ripened by heavenly rays,
  be harvested to my joy and thy praise.
Help me to gain profit by what I read,
  as treasure beyond all treasure,
  a fountain which can replenish my dry heart,
   its waters flowing through me as a perennial river
   on-drawn by thy Holy Spirit.
Enable me to distil from its pages faithful prayer
  that grasps the arm of thy omnipotence,
  achieves wonders, obtains blessings,
  and draws down streams of mercy.
From it show me how my words have often been unfaithful to thee,
  injurious to my fellow-men,
  empty of grace, full of folly,
  dishonouring to my calling.
Then write thy own words upon my heart and inscribe them on my
  lips;
So shall all glory be to thee in my reading of thy Word!

A MINISTER'S PREACHING

MY MASTER GOD,
I am desired to preach today,
    but go weak and needy to my task;
Yet I long that people might be edified with divine truth,
    that an honest testimony might be borne for thee;
Give me assistance in preaching and prayer,
    with heart uplifted for grace and unction.
Present to my view things pertinent to my subject,
    with fullness of matter and clarity of thought,
    proper expressions, fluency, fervency,
    a feeling sense of the things I preach,
    and grace to apply them to men's consciences.
Keep me conscious all the while of my defects,
    and let me not gloat in pride over my performance.
Help me to offer a testimony for thyself,
    and to leave sinners inexcusable in neglecting thy mercy.
Give me freedom to open the sorrows of thy people,
    and to set before them comforting considerations.
Attend with power the truth preached,
    and awaken the attention of my slothful audience.
May thy people be refreshed, melted, convicted, comforted,
    and help me to use the strongest arguments
    drawn from Christ's incarnation and sufferings,
    that men might be made holy.

I myself need thy support, comfort, strength, holiness,
    that I might be a pure channel of thy grace,
    and be able to do something for thee;
Give me then refreshment among thy people,
    and help me not to treat excellent matter in a defective way,
    or bear a broken testimony to so worthy a redeemer,
    or be harsh in treating of Christ's death, its design and end,
      from lack of warmth and fervency.
And keep me in tune with thee as I do this work.

SCRIPTURAL CONVICTIONS

O GOD OF LOVE,
I approach thee with encouragements derived from thy character,
    for I am not left to feel after thee in the darkness of my nature,
        nor to worship thee as the unknown God.
I cannot find out thy perfections, but I know thou art good,
    ready to forgive, plenteous in mercy.
Thou hast displayed thy wisdom, power, and goodness in all thy
    works,
    and hast revealed thy will in the Scripture of truth.
Thou hast caused it to be preserved, translated, published, multiplied,
    so that all men may possess it and find thee in it.
Here I see thy greatness and thy grace,
       thy pity and thy rectitude,
       thy mercy and thy truth,
       thy being and men's hearts;
Through it thou hast magnified thy name,
    and favoured mankind with the gospel.
Have mercy on me,
   for I have ungratefully received thy benefits,
      little improved my privileges,
      made light of spiritual things,
      disregarded thy messages,
      contended with examples of the good,
            rebukes of conscience,
            admonitions of friends,
            leadings of providence.
I deserve that thy kingdom be taken away from me.
Lord, I confess my sin with feeling, lamentation, a broken heart,
    a contrite spirit, self-abhorrence, self-condemnation,
      self-despair.
Give me relief by Jesus my hope,
    faith in his name of Saviour,
    forgiveness by his blood,
    strength by his presence,
    holiness by his Spirit:
And let me love thee with all my heart.

GOD OF THE PASSING HOUR,
Another week has gone and I have been preserved
    in my going out,
    in my coming in.
Thine has been the vigilance that has turned threatened evils aside;
Thine the supplies that have nourished me;
Thine the comforts that have indulged me;
Thine the relations and friends that have delighted me;
Thine the means of grace which have edified me;
Thine the Book, which, amidst all my enjoyments,
    has told me that this is not my rest,
    that in all successes one thing alone is needful,
    to love my Saviour.
Nothing can equal the number of thy mercies
    but my imperfections and sins.
These, O God, I will neither conceal nor palliate,
    but confess with a broken heart.
In what condition would secret reviews of my life leave me
    were it not for the assurance that with thee
    there is plenteous redemption,
    that thou art a forgiving God,
    that thou mayest be feared!
While I hope for pardon through the blood of the cross,
    I pray to be clothed with humility,
    to be quickened in thy way,
    to be more devoted to thee,
    to keep the end of my life in view,
    to be cured of the folly of delay and indecision,
    to know how frail I am,
    to number my days and apply my heart unto
      wisdom.

THE LORD'S DAY

O LORD MY LORD,
   this is thy day,
   the heavenly ordinance of rest,
   the open door of worship,
   the record of Jesus' resurrection,
   the seal of the sabbath to come,
   the day when saints militant and triumphant unite in endless song.
I bless thee for the throne of grace,
        that here free favour reigns;
         that open access to it is through the blood of Jesus;
         that the veil is torn aside and I can enter the holiest
           and find thee ready to hear,
                waiting to be gracious,
                inviting me to pour out my needs,
                encouraging my desires,
                promising to give more than I ask or think.
But while I bless thee, shame and confusion are mine:
      I remember my past misuse of sacred things,
          my irreverent worship,
          my base ingratitude,
          my cold, dull praise.
Sprinkle all my past sabbaths with the cleansing blood of Jesus,
      and may this day witness deep improvement in me.
Give me in rich abundance
      the blessings the Lord's Day was designed to impart;
May my heart be fast bound against worldly thoughts or cares;
Flood my mind with peace beyond understanding;
      may my meditations be sweet,
         my acts of worship life, liberty, joy,
         my drink the streams that flow from thy throne,
         my food the precious Word,
         my defence the shield of faith,
          and may my heart be more knit to Jesus.

LORD'S DAY MORNING

O MAKER AND UPHOLDER OF ALL THINGS,
  Day and night are thine; they are also mine from thee—
    the night to rid me of the cares of the day,
        to refresh my weary body,
        to renew my natural strength;
    the day to summon me to new activities,
        to give me opportunity to glorify thee,
        to serve my generation,
        to acquire knowledge, holiness, eternal life.
But one day above all days is made especially
  for thy honour and my improvement;
The sabbath reminds me of thy rest from creation,
            of the resurrection of my saviour,
            of his entering into repose,
Thy house is mine,
    but I am unworthy to meet thee there,
    and am unfit for spiritual service.
When I enter it I come before thee as a sinner,
    condemned by conscience and thy Word,
For I am still in the body and in the wilderness,
    ignorant, weak, in danger,
    and in need of thine aid.
But encouraged by thy all-sufficient grace
    let me go to thy house with a lively hope of meeting thee,
    knowing that there thou wilt come to me and give me peace.
My soul is drawn out to thee in longing desires
    for thy presence in the sanctuary, at the table,
    where all are entertained on a feast of good things;
Let me before the broken elements, emblems of thy dying love,
    cry to thee with broken heart for grace and forgiveness.
I long for that blissful communion of thy people
    in thy eternal house in the perfect kingdom;
    These are they that follow the Lamb;
May I be of their company!

WORSHIP

GLORIOUS GOD,
It is the flame of my life to worship thee,
    the crown and glory of my soul to adore thee,
    heavenly pleasure to approach thee.
Give me power by thy Spirit to help me worship now,
      that I may forget the world,
          be brought into fullness of life,
          be refreshed, comforted, blessed.
Give me knowledge of thy goodness
      that I might not be over-awed by thy greatness;
Give me Jesus, Son of Man, Son of God,
      that I might not be terrified,
      but be drawn near with filial love,
          with holy boldness;
He is my mediator, brother, interpreter,
      branch, daysman, Lamb;
      him I glorify,
      in him I am set on high.
Crowns to give I have none,
      but what thou hast given I return,
      content to feel that everything is mine when it is thine,
      and the more fully mine when I have yielded it to thee.
Let me live wholly to my Saviour,
      free from distractions,
      from carking care,
      from hindrances to the pursuit of the narrow way.
I am pardoned through the blood of Jesus—
      give me a new sense of it,
      continue to pardon me by it,
      may I come every day to the fountain,
      and every day be washed anew,
      that I may worship thee always in spirit and truth.

THE LORD'S SUPPER

GOD OF ALL GOOD,
I bless thee for the means of grace;
  teach me to see in them thy loving purposes
  and the joy and strength of my soul.
Thou hast prepared for me a feast;
and though I am unworthy to sit down as guest,
I wholly rest on the merits of Jesus,
  and hide myself beneath his righteousness;
When I hear his tender invitation
  and see his wondrous grace,
   I cannot hesitate, but must come to thee in love.
By thy Spirit enliven my faith rightly to discern
  and spiritually to apprehend the Saviour.
While I gaze upon the emblems of my Saviour's death,
  may I ponder why he died, and hear him say,
   'I gave my life to purchase yours,
    presented myself an offering to expiate your sin,
    shed my blood to blot out your guilt,
    opened my side to make you clean,
    endured your curses to set you free,
    bore your condemnation to satisfy divine justice.'
O may I rightly grasp the breadth and length of this design,
  draw near, obey, extend the hand, take the bread,
  receive the cup, eat and drink,
  testify before all men that I do for myself,
  gladly, in faith, reverence and love, receive my Lord,
  to be my life, strength, nourishment, joy, delight.
In the supper I remember his eternal love, boundless grace,
  infinite compassion, agony, cross, redemption,
  and receive assurance of pardon, adoption, life, glory.
As the outward elements nourish my body,
  so may thy indwelling Spirit invigorate my soul,
  until that day when I hunger and thirst no more,
  and sit with Jesus at his heavenly feast.

THE MINISTER BEFORE SACRAMENT

LORD,
Teach me the nature of a sacrament as a seal and pledge of love,
    that Christ is faithful to make himself
    a present reality to his own who are guests at his table.
Assure me by it
      that his word is made good to my faith,
      that he by sacramental union is given to me,
      that I shall have strength not to fall into sin,
      that his life begun in me will be perfected hereafter,
      that my covenant with him is confirmed,
      that he gives himself to all who take him thankfully.
As I come to the feast, help me to recall
      my neglect of duties towards myself,
        my family, church, friends,
          by not instructing, exhorting, being an example.
Grant me to see my ignorance, not knowing how or what to pray,
        my unsavouriness, not delighting in,
          but loathing to speak for thee,
        my pride, because I would not speak what I could
          from fear of not doing it well,
        my lukewarmness, in not reaching for thy glory,
        my idleness and sloth,
        my want of tender love,
        my apprehension of unfruitfulness
          in case I should attempt and do no good,
          and hence sow seed upon rocks.
Let me know that even if I have done right,
      yet I must lament the principles that caused my neglect,
      that good duties might be done or omitted
        out of ill principles or motives,
        and only when these are dealt with shall I know
        what is my duty and its extent.
Heal me now, as I approach thy table,
      and fill me with all grace, with thyself.

LORD'S DAY EVENING

MOST HOLY GOD,
May the close of an earthly sabbath
  remind me that the last of them will one day end.
Animate me with joy that in heaven praise will never cease,
  that adoration will continue for ever,
  that no flesh will grow weary,
    no congregations disperse,
    no affections flag,
    no thoughts wander,
    no will droop,
    but all will be adoring love.
Guard my mind from making ordinances my stay or trust,
    from hewing out broken cisterns,
    from resting on outward helps.
Wing me through earthly forms to thy immediate presence;
May my feeble prayers show me the emptiness and vanity of my sins;
Deepen in me the conviction that my most fervent prayers,
  and most lowly confessions, need to be repented of.
May my best services bring me nearer to the cross,
  and prompt me to cry, 'None but Jesus!'
By thy Spirit give abiding life to the lessons of this day:
May the seed sown take deep root and yield a full harvest.
Let all who see me take knowledge that I have been with thee
  that thou hast taught me my need as a sinner,
    hast revealed a finished salvation to me,
    hast enriched me with all spiritual blessings,
    hast chosen me to show forth Jesus to others,
    hast helped me to dispel the mists of unbelief.
O great creator, mighty protector, gracious preserver,
  thou dost load me with lovingkindnesses,
  and hast made me thy purchased possession,
  and redeemed me from all guilt;
I praise and bless thee for my sabbath rest, my calm conscience,
    my peace of heart.

THE MINISTER'S COVENANT

LORD JESUS,
True God, everlasting Life, redeemer of sinners,
        I give my body, soul, intellect, will, affections to thee.
I call the day, sun, earth, trees, stones, wind, rain, frost, snow,
        my home, bed, table, food, books, drink, clothes,
        to witness that I come to thee for rest of soul
          from the thunders of guilt and dread of eternity.
Grant me a circumcised heart that I may love thee,
        a right spirit that I may seek thy glory,
        a principle within which thou wilt own,
        an interest in the blood that cleanses,
          the righteousness that justifies,
          the redemption that delivers,
      that I may not be found a hypocrite on Judgment Day.
For the sake of thy cruel death
        take my time, strength, gifts, talents, usefulness, piety,
        which in full purpose of heart I consecrate to thee.
Let not sin find a place in my heart to becloud my vision,
        and may no foolish act wither my gifts.
Preserve me from the falls by which others stumble,
        that thy name may not be blasphemed or wounded,
        that thy people may not be grieved,
        that thine enemies may not be hardened,
        that my peace may not be injured.
Give me a heart full of love to thyself and to others.
Let me discover in this life what I am before thee
        that I may not find myself another character hereafter.
Prepare me for death,
        that I may not die after long affliction or suddenly,
        but after short illness, with no confusion or disorder,
        and a quiet discharge in peace, with adieu to brethren.
Let not my days end like lumber in a house,
        but give me a silent removing from one world to another.
Inscribe these petitions in thy book, present them to thy Father,
Set thine *Amen* to them as I do on my part of the covenant.

IX
Valediction

EARTH AND HEAVEN

O LORD,
I live here as a fish in a vessel of water,
   only enough to keep me alive,
    but in heaven I shall swim in the ocean.
Here I have a little air in me to keep me breathing,
    but there I shall have sweet and fresh gales;
Here I have a beam of sun to lighten my darkness,
    a warm ray to keep me from freezing;
    yonder I shall live in light and warmth for ever.
My natural desires are corrupt and misguided,
    and it is thy mercy to destroy them;
My spiritual longings are of thy planting,
    and thou wilt water and increase them;
Quicken my hunger and thirst after the realm above.
Here I can have the world,
    there I shall have thee in Christ;
Here is a life of longing and prayer,
    there is assurance without suspicion,
          asking without refusal;
Here are gross comforts, more burden than benefit,
    there is joy without sorrow,
        comfort without suffering,
        love without inconstancy,
        rest without weariness.
Give me to know that heaven is all love,
    where the eye affects the heart,
    and the continual viewing of thy beauty
    keeps the soul in continual transports of delight.
Give me to know that heaven is all peace,
    where error, pride, rebellion, passion raise no head.
Give me to know that heaven is all joy,
    the end of believing, fasting, praying, mourning,
    humbling, watching, fearing, repining;
And lead me to it soon.

HEAVEN DESIRED

O MY LORD,

   May I arrive where means of grace cease
      and I need no more to fast, pray, weep, watch,
      be tempted, attend preaching and sacrament;
      where nothing defiles,
      where is no grief, sorrow, sin, death, separation, tears,
        pale face, languid body, aching joints, feeble infancy,
        decrepit age, peccant humours, pining sickness,
        griping fears, consuming cares;
      where is personal completeness;
      where the more perfect the sight the more beautiful the object,
          the more perfect the appetite the sweeter the food,
          the more musical the ear the more pleasant the melody,
          the more complete the soul the more happy its joys,
      where is full knowledge of thee.
Here I am an ant, and as I view a nest of ants
      so dost thou view me and my fellow-creatures;
But as an ant knows not me, my nature, my thoughts,
      so here I cannot know thee clearly,
But there I shall be near thee,
              dwell with thy family,
              stand in thy presence chamber,
              be an heir of thy kingdom,
                as the spouse of Christ,
                as a member of his body,
                one with him who is one with thee,
              and exercise all my powers of body and soul
              in the enjoyment of thee.
As praise in the mouth of thy saints is comely,
      so teach me to exercise this divine gift,
      when I pray, read, hear, see, do,
      in the presence of people and of my enemies,
      as I hope to praise thee eternally hereafter.

RETROSPECT AND PROSPECT

SUPREME RULER OF THE VISIBLE AND INVISIBLE WORLDS,
My heart is drawn out to thee
      for thy amazing grace and condescension.
Thou hast kept my conversion fresh before me,
      that season of my first spiritual comfort
      when I passed through the Red Sea
      by a way I did not expect.
I rejoiced then for that unthought-of passage,
      that delivered me from the fear of the Egyptian
      when I had almost despaired of life.
I rejoice now as these things are fresh and lively in my mind.
My soul melts when I think of thy days of old with me,
      when a poor worthless creature
      without wisdom to direct or strength to help myself
      was laid under the happy necessity
      of living upon thee and finding thy consolations large.
Thou art my divine treasury in whom all fullness dwells,
      my life, hope, joy, peace, glory, end;
May I be daily more and more conformed to thee,
      with the meekness and calmness of the Lamb in my soul,
      and a feeling sense of the felicity of heaven,
      where I long to join angels free from imperfections,
      where in me the image of my adored Saviour
          will be completely restored,
      so that I may be fit for his enjoyments and employments.
I am not afraid to look the king of terrors in the face,
      for I know I shall be drawn, not driven, out of the world.
Until then let me continually glow and burn out for thee,
      and when the last great change shall come
      let me awake in thy likeness,
      leaving behind me an example that will glorify thee
      while my spirit rejoices in heaven,
      and my memory is blessed upon earth,
      with those who follow me praising thee for my life.

X
A Week's Shared Prayers

FIRST DAY MORNING
WORSHIP

O LORD,
We commune with thee every day,
    but week days are worldly days,
    and secular concerns reduce heavenly impressions.
We bless thee therefore for the day sacred to our souls
    when we can wait upon thee and be refreshed;
We thank thee for the institutions of religion
    by use of which we draw near to thee and thou to us;
We rejoice in another Lord's Day
    when we call off our minds from the cares of the world
    and attend upon thee without distraction;
Let our retirement be devout,
    our conversation edifying,
    our reading pious,
    our hearing profitable,
      that our souls may be quickened and elevated.
We are going to the house of prayer,
    pour upon us the spirit of grace and supplication;
We are going to the house of praise,
    awaken in us every grateful and cheerful emotion;
We are going to the house of instruction,
    give testimony to the Word preached,
    and glorify it in the hearts of all who hear;
    may it enlighten the ignorant,
        awaken the careless, reclaim the wandering,
        establish the weak, comfort the feeble-minded,
        make ready a people for their Lord.

Be a sanctuary to all who cannot come,
Forget not those who never come,
And do thou bestow upon us
    benevolence towards our dependents,
    forgiveness towards our enemies,
    peaceableness towards our neighbours,
    openness towards our fellow-Christians.

FIRST DAY EVENING

THE TEACHER

O GOD,
We bless thee,
   our creator, preserver, benefactor, teacher,
      for opening to us the volume of nature
      where we may read and consider thy works.
Thou hast this day spread before us the fuller pages of revelation,
      and in them we see what thou wouldest have us do,
                  what thou requirest of us,
                  what thou hast done for us,
                  what thou hast promised to us,
                  what thou hast given us in Jesus.
We pray thee for a conscious experience of his salvation,
   in our deliverance from sin,
   in our bearing his image,
   in our enjoying his presence,
   in our being upheld by his free Spirit.
Let us not live uncertain of what we are,
              of where we are going.
Bear witness with our spirit that we are thy children;
And enable each one to say, 'I know my redeemer.'
Bless us with a growing sense of this salvation.
If already enlightened in Christ, may we see greater things;
If quickened, may we have more abundant life;
If renewed, let us go on from strength to strength.
Give us closer abiding in Jesus that we may
   bring forth more fruit,
   have a deeper sense of our obligations to him,
      that we may surrender all,
   have a fuller joy,
      that we may serve him more completely.
And may our faith work by love
   towards him who died,
   towards our fellow-believers,
   towards our fellow-men.

SECOND DAY MORNING

GOD OVER ALL

O GOD ALL-SUFFICIENT,
Thou hast made and upholdest all things by the word of thy power;
>> darkness is thy pavilion,
>> thou walkest on the wings of the wind;
>> all nations are nothing before thee;
>> one generation succeeds another,
>> and we hasten back to the dust;
>> the heavens we behold will vanish away
>>> like the clouds that cover them,
>> the earth we tread on will dissolve
>>> as a morning dream;
But thou, unchangeable and incorruptible,
>> art for ever and ever,
>> God over all, blessed eternally.
Infinitely great and glorious art thou.
We are thy offspring and thy care.
Thy hands have made and fashioned us.
Thou hast watched over us with more than parental love,
>>>>> more than maternal tenderness.
Thou hast holden our soul in life,
> and not suffered our feet to be moved.
Thy divine power has given us all things
> necessary for life and godliness.
Let us bless thee at all times and forget not how thou hast
>> forgiven our iniquities,
>> healed our diseases,
>> redeemed our lives from destruction,
>> crowned us with lovingkindness and tender mercies,
>> satisfied our mouths with good things,
>> renewed our youth like the eagle's.
May thy Holy Scriptures
> govern every part of our lives,
> and regulate the discharge of all our duties,
> so that we may adorn thy doctrine in all things.

[211]

SECOND DAY EVENING

BOUNTY

THOU GREAT AND ONLY POTENTATE,
Thou hast made summer and winter, day and night;
    each of these revolutions serves our welfare
    and is full of thy care and kindness.
Thy bounty is seen
    in the relations that train us,
      the laws that defend us,
      the homes that shelter us,
      the food that builds us,
      the raiment that comforts us,
      the continuance of our health, members, senses,
        understanding, memory, affection, will.
But as stars fade before the rising sun,
    thou hast eclipsed all these benefits
    in the wisdom and grace that purposed
    redemption by Jesus thy Son.
Blessed be thy mercy that laid help on
    one that is mighty and willing,
    one that is able to save to the uttermost.
Make us deeply sensible of our need of his saving grace,
                of the blood that cleanses,
                of the rest he has promised,
And impute to us that righteousness which justifies the guilty,
    gives them a title to eternal life,
    and possession of the Spirit.
May we love the freeness of salvation, and joy in its holiness;
Give us faith to grasp thy promises, that are our hope,
    provide for every exigency, and prevent every evil;
Keep our hearts from straying after forbidden pleasures;
May thy will bind all our wishes;
Let us live out of the world as to its spirit, maxim, manners,
    but live in it as the sphere of our action and usefulness;
May we be alive to every call of duty, accepting without question
    thy determination of our circumstances and our service.

THIRD DAY MORNING

GOD CREATOR AND CONTROLLER

MOST HIGH GOD,
The universe with all its myriad creatures is thine,
    made by thy word, upheld by thy power, governed by thy will.
But thou art also the Father of mercies,
        the God of all grace,
        the bestower of all comfort,
        the protector of the saved.
Thou hast been mindful of us,
    hast visited us, preserved us,
        given us a goodly heritage—
            the Holy Scriptures,
            the joyful gospel,
            the saviour of souls,
We come to thee in Jesus' name,
    make mention of his righteousness only,
    plead his obedience and sufferings
        who magnified the law both in its precepts and penalty,
        and made it honourable.
May we be justified by his blood,
        saved by his life,
        joined to his Spirit.
Let us take up his cross and follow him.
May the agency of thy grace prepare us for thy dispensations.
Make us willing that thou shouldest choose our inheritance and
    determine what we shall retain or lose, suffer or enjoy;
If blessed with prosperity may we be free from its snares,
    and use, not abuse, its advantages;
May we patiently and cheerfully submit to those afflictions
    which are necessary.
When we are tempted to wander, hedge up our way,
                excite in us abhorrence of sin,
                wean us from the present evil world,
Assure us that we shall at last enter Immanuel's land
    where none is ever sick, and the sun will always shine.

THIRD DAY EVENING

BEFORE SLEEP

GOD OF ALL SOVEREIGNTY,
Thy greatness is unsearchable,
Thy name most excellent,
Thy glory above the heavens;
Ten thousand minister to thee,
Ten thousand times ten thousand stand before thee;
In thy awful presence we are less than nothing.
We do not approach thee because we deserve thy notice,
    for we are sinners;

        Our necessities compel us,
        Thy promises encourage us,
        Our broken hearts incite us,
        The mediator draws us,
        Thy acceptance of others moves us.

Look thou upon us and be merciful unto us;
Convince us of the penalty and pollution of sin;
Give us faith to believe, and, believing, to have life in Jesus;
May we enter into his sufferings;
Let us see thy hand in the instruments of our grief,
    rejoicing that they are from thy over-ruling providence.
Let not our weeping hinder sowing; nor sorrow, duty.
While living in a world of change let us seek the abiding city.
Be with us to our journey's end
    that we may glorify thee in death as in life.
We bless thee for preservation, supplies, mercies,
    and to thee, keeper of souls, we commit all we are and have.
May no evil befall us, no sickness come nigh us,
    no horror disturb us!
May our conscience be clear, our hearts pure, our sleep sweet!
And with the innumerable company who neither slumber nor rest
    we join in ascribing blessing, honour, glory and power
    to the Lamb upon the throne, for ever and ever.

FOURTH DAY MORNING

TRUE CHRISTIANITY

LORD OF HEAVEN,
Thy goodness is inexpressible and inconceivable.
In the works of creation thou art almighty,
In the dispensations of providence all-wise,
In the gospel of grace all love,
And in thy Son thou hast provided for
      our deliverance from the effects of sin,
      the justification of our persons,
      the sanctification of our natures,
      the perseverance of our souls in the path of life.
Though exposed to the terrors of thy law,
      we have a refuge, from the storm;
Though compelled to cry, 'Unclean,'
      we have a fountain for sin;
Though creature-cells of emptiness
      we have a fullness accessible to all,
      and incapable of reduction.
Grant us always to know that to walk with Jesus
      makes other interests a shadow and a dream.
Keep us from intermittent attention to eternal things;
Save us from the delusion of those
      who fail to go far in religion,
      who are concerned but not converted,
      who have another heart but not a new one,
      who have light, zeal, confidence, but not Christ.
Let us judge our Christianity, not only by our dependence upon Jesus,
      but by our love to him,
         our conformity to him,
         our knowledge of him.
Give us a religion that is both real and progressive,
         that holds on its way and grows stronger,
         that lives and works in the Spirit,
         that profits by every correction,
         and is injured by no carnal indulgence.

FOURTH DAY EVENING

GOD ALL-SUFFICIENT

KING OF GLORY, DIVINE MAJESTY,
Every perfection adorns thy nature and sustains thy throne;
The heavens and earth are thine,
The world is thine and its fullness.
Thy power created the universe from nothing;
Thy wisdom has managed all its multiple concerns,
    presiding over nations, families, individuals.
Thy goodness is boundless;
    all creatures wait on thee
            are supplied by thee,
            are satisfied in thee.
How precious are the thoughts of thy mercy and grace!
How excellent thy lovingkindness that draws men to thee!

Teach us to place our happiness in thee, the blessed God,
    never seeking life among the dead things of earth,
    or asking for that which satisfies the deluded;
But may we prize the light of thy smile,
        implore the joy of thy salvation,
        find our heaven in thee.
Thou hast attended to our happiness more than we can do;
Though we are fallen creatures thou hast not neglected us.
In love and pity thou hast provided us a saviour;
Apply his redemption to our hearts,
    by justifying our persons,
    and sanctifying our natures.
We confess our transgressions, have mercy on us.
We are weary, give us rest,
     ignorant, make us wise unto salvation,
     helpless, let thy strength be made perfect in our weakness,
     poor and needy, bless us with Christ's unsearchable riches,
     perplexed and tempted, let us travel on unchecked,
       undismayed,
         knowing that thou hast said,
       'I will never leave thee nor forsake thee'.
Blessed be thy name!

FIFTH DAY MORNING

THE GIVER

CREATOR, UPHOLDER AND PROPRIETOR OF ALL THINGS,
We cannot escape from thy presence and control,
  nor do we desire to do so.
Our privilege is to be under the agency of thy omnipotence,
  righteousness, wisdom, patience, mercy and grace;
For thou art Love with more than parental affection.
We admire thy goodness,
  stand in awe of thy power,
  abase ourselves before thy purity.
It is the discovery of thy goodness alone that
  can banish our fear
  allure us into thy presence,
  help us to bewail and confess our sins.
We review our past guilt
  and are conscious of present unworthiness.
We bless thee that thy steadfast love and attributes
  are essential to our happiness and hope;
Thou hast witnessed to us thy grace and mercy
    in the bounties of nature,
    in the fullness of thy providence,
    in the revelations of Scripture,
    in the gift of thy Son,
    in the proclamation of the gospel.
Make us willing to be saved in thy own way,
  perceiving nothing in ourselves but all in Jesus.
Help us not only to receive him but
      to walk in him,
      depend upon him,
      commune with him,
      follow him as dear children,
    imperfect, but still pressing forward,
    not complaining of labour, but valuing rest,
    not murmuring under trials, but thankful for our state.
And by so doing let us silence the ignorance of foolish men.

FIFTH DAY EVENING

PROTECTION

O LORD GOD,
Thou art our preserver, governor, saviour,
    and coming judge.
Quieten our souls to call upon thy name;
Detach us from the influence of the flesh and the senses;
Impress us with the power of faith;
Promote in us spirituality of mind
    that will render our services acceptable to thee,
    and delightful and profitable to ourselves.
Bring us into that state which attracts thine eye,
    and prepare us to receive the proofs of thy love.
Show us our danger, that we may fly to thee for refuge.
Make us sensible of our sin's disease, that we may value the good
    physician.
Placard to us the cross, that it may slay the enmity of our hearts.
Help us to be watchful over our ways,
              jealous over our tempers,
              diligent over our hearts.
When we droop, revive us,
          When we loiter, quicken us,
          When we go astray, restore us.
Possess us with more of that faith
    which is the principle of all vital godliness.
May we be rich in faith,
          strong in faith,
          live by faith,
          walk by faith,
          experience the joy of faith,
          do the work of faith,
          hope through faith.
Perceiving nothing in ourselves,
    may we find in the Saviour
    wisdom, righteousness, sanctification, redemption.

SIXTH DAY MORNING
THE GOSPEL

O THOU MOST HIGH,
Creator of the ends of the earth,
Governor of the universe,
Judge of all men,
Head of the church,
Saviour of sinners;

        thy greatness is unsearchable,
        thy goodness infinite,
        thy compassions unfailing,
        thy providence boundless,
        thy mercies ever new.

We bless thee for the words of salvation.
How important, suitable, encouraging
    are the doctrines, promises, and invitations
    of the gospel of peace!
We are lost: but in it thou hast presented to us
    a full, free and eternal salvation;
      weak: but here we learn that help is found in one that is mighty,
      poor: but in him we discover unsearchable riches,
      blind: but we find he has treasures of wisdom and knowledge.
We thank thee for thy unspeakable gift.
Thy Son is our only refuge, foundation, hope, confidence;
We depend upon his death,
    rest in his righteousness,
    desire to bear his image;
May his glory fill our minds,
    his love reign in our affections,
    his cross inflame us with ardour.
Let us as Christians fill our various situations in life,
        escape the snares to which they expose us,
        discharge the duties that arise from our
          circumstances,
        enjoy with moderation their advantages,
        improve with diligence their usefulness,
And may every place and company we are in be benefited by us.

SIXTH DAY EVENING

THE MEDIATOR

O GOD OF ABRAHAM, ISAAC AND JACOB,
We hope in thy Word.
   There we see thee, not on a fearful throne of judgment
   But on a throne of grace
      waiting to be gracious, and exalted in mercy.
   There we hear thee saying, not 'Depart ye cursed,' but
    'Look unto me and be ye saved,
       for I am God and there is none else.'
They that know thy name put their trust in thee.
   How many now glorified in heaven, and what numbers living on
    earth,
    are thy witnesses, O God,
      exemplifying in their recovery from the ruins of the fall
        the freeness, riches and efficacy of thy grace!
All that were ever saved were saved by thee,
      and will through eternity exclaim, 'Not unto us, but
      unto thy name give glory for thy mercy and truth's sake.'
Thou hast chosen to transact all thy concerns with us
    through a mediator in whom all fullness dwells
    and who is exalted to be prince and saviour.
To him we look, on him we depend, through him we are
    justified.

May we derive relief from his sufferings
        without ceasing to abhor sin,
        or to long after holiness;
    feel the double efficacy of his blood,
      tranquillizing and cleansing our consciences;
    delight in his service as well as in his sacrifice;
    be constrained by his love
      to live not to ourselves but to him;
    cherish a grateful and cheerful disposition,
    not murmuring and repining if our wishes are not indulged,
    or because some trials are blended with our enjoyments,

But, sensible of our desert,
    and impressed with the number and greatness of thy
      benefits,
    may we bless and praise thee at all times.

SEVENTH DAY MORNING

GOD'S GOOD PLEASURE

SOVEREIGN LORD,
Thy will is supreme in heaven and earth,
    and all beings are creatures of thy power.
Thou art the Father of our spirits;
        thy inspiration gives us understanding,
        thy providence governs our lives.
But, O God, we are sinners in thy sight;
        thou hast judged us so,
        and if we deny it we make thee a liar.
Yet in Christ thou art reconciled to thy rebellious subjects;
        give us the ear of faith to hear him,
                the eye of faith to see him,
                the hand of faith to receive him,
                the appetite of faith to feed upon him;
                    that we might find in him light,
                    riches, honour, eternal life.
Thou art the inviting one, may we hearken to thee;
            the almighty instructor, teach us to live to thee;
            the light-dweller, inaccessible to man and angels,
                hiding thyself behind the elements of creation,
                but known to us in Jesus,
Possess our minds with the grandeur of thy perfections.
Thy love to us in Jesus is firm and changeless,
        nothing can separate us from it,
        and in the enjoyment of it nothing can make us miserable.
Preserve us from hypocrisy and formality in religion;
Enable us to remember what thou art and what we are,
        to recall thy holiness and our unworthiness;
Help us to approach thee clothed with humility,
        for vanity, forwardness, insensibility,
        disorderly affection, backwardness to duty,
        proneness to evil are in our hearts.
Let us never forget thy patience, wisdom, power, faithfulness, care,
        and never cease to respond to thy invitations.

SEVENTH DAY EVENING

FUTURE BLESSINGS

O LORD GOD,
There is no blessing we implore but thou art able to give,
    hast promised to give,
    hast given already to countless multitudes,
    all unworthy and guilty like ourselves;
Make us willing to receive the supply of our need from thy bounty.
To this end convince us of sin,
    soften our hard hearts,
    to bewail our folly, ingratitude, pride,
        unbelief, rebellion, corruption.
Through the law may we die to the law,
    then look with wonder, submission, delight,
    to the provision thou hast made for the glory of thy name
        in the salvation of sinners.
Give us a hope that makes us not ashamed,
    a love that excites to holy obedience,
    a joy in thee that is our strength,
    a faith in thy Son who loved us and died for us.
May we persevere in duty when not fully conscious of thee,
    wait upon thee and keep thy way,
    be humble and earnest suppliants at thy feet,
    live continually as on the brink of eternity.
Let us be at thy disposal for the duties and events of life,
    submit our preferences to thy wisdom and will,
    resign our enjoyments if thou shouldest require it
    as our absolute proprietor and best friend.
In our unworthiness and provocations make us grateful,
    for the means of grace and the ordinances of religion
    and teach us to profit by them more than we have done.
Help us to be in the Spirit on the Lord's Day,
    to enter upon the sabbath mindful of its solemnities, duties,
      privileges,
    setting all things worldly aside while we worship thee.
May we know the blessedness of men whose strength is in thee,
    and in whose hearts are the highways to heaven.

Bibliography

BAXTER, RICHARD, *The Saint's Rest.*

BRAINERD, DAVID, *Diary, Journal and Letters*, Melrose 1902.

BUNYAN, JOHN, *Grace Abounding*, London 1893.

DODDRIDGE, PHILIP, *The Rise and Progress of Religion in the Soul*, London 1892.

EVANS, CHRISTMAS, *Life of*, by Paxton Hood, London 1902.

JAY, WILLIAM, *Prayers for the Use of Families*, London 1840.

LAW, HENRY, *Family Prayers*, London 1869.

ROMAINE, WILLIAM, *The Walk of Faith*, London 1819.

SHEPARD, THOMAS, *Works*, Vol. 3, Boston U.S.A. 1853.

SPURGEON, CHARLES HADDON, *The Pastor in Prayer*, Pasadena U.S.A. 1971.

TOPLADY, AUGUSTUS M., *Works*, Vol. 1, London 1825.

WATSON, THOMAS, *The Lord's Prayer*, London 1960.

WATTS, ISAAC, *Works*, Vol. 3, Section 'A Guide to Prayer.' London 1810.

WILLIAMS, WILLIAM, Free translations from *Y Caniedydd Cynulleidfaol Newydd*, Swansea 1921.

The Editor is responsible for the titles, ascriptions, and structure of the prayers in this present volume, and for the introductory prayer, 'The Valley of Vision'.